P9-ELW-564

25 SKI TOURS IN VERMONT

From Backcountry Wilderness to Cross-Country Ski Centers

Stan Wass

A 25 SKI TOURS™ BOOK

Backcountry Publications
The Countryman Press, Inc.
Woodstock, Vermont

An Invitation to the Reader—
With time, trails may be rerouted and signs and landmarks
altered. If you find that changes have occurred on the routes
described in this book, please let the author and publisher
know so that corrections may be made in future editions. Other
comments and suggestions are also welcome. Address all
correspondence to:

Editor, 25 Ski Tours℠
Backcountry Publications
P.O. Box 175
Woodstock, VT 05091

Library of Congress Cataloging-in-Publication Data
Wass, Stan.
    25 ski tours in Vermont : from backcountry wilderness to cross
-country ski centers / by Stan Wass.
        p.   cm.—(A Twenty-five ski tours book)
    ISBN 0-88150-114-X
    1. Cross-country skiing—Vermont—Guide-books.   2. Ski resorts—
Vermont—Guide-books.   3. Vermont—Description and travel—1981—
Vermont.   III. Series: 25 ski tours book.
GV854.5.V5W37   1990
796.93'2—dc20

                                                        90-45227
                                                        CIP

© 1990 by Stan Wass
All rights reserved

Published by Backcountry Publications
A division of The Countryman Press, Inc.
Woodstock, VT 05091

Photo Credits:
Page 15 by Rolf Anderson; page 24 by The Bennington
Banner; page 51 by Viking Ski Touring Centre; page 66 by
Janet Upton; pages 129, 150, and 151 by John Brodhead;
page 145 by Jan Reynolds/Stowe Photo. All other photos by
Stan Wass.

Cover design and text layout by Virginia L. Scott
Maps by Richard Widhu, © 1990 by The Countryman Press, Inc.
Printed in the United States of America

Dedication

I dedicate this book to my wife, Jane, who died while
the project was still in the planning stages. She made it
all possible.

I thank Jane's mother, Ethel Colburn, Jane's brother,
Les, and his family, Devra, Jesse, Jon, and Jeniffer, for
helping me through some tough times.

Acknowledgements

This book could not have been written without a great
deal of help, and I can thank here only some of the people who provided assistance. Wendy Williams skied with
me, posed for pictures, and helped keep the project
going. Ed Eveleth and Geoff Dickson also posed for a
lot of pictures and skied some tough backcountry tours
with me. Area operators and staff were particularly helpful: Don Cochrane at Mt. Meadows, Stan Swaim at
Burke, John Brodhead at Craftsbury, John Wiggin at
Woodstock, Rolf Anderson at Hazen's Notch, Tony Clark
at Blueberry Hill, and many others contributed invaluable
information.

Finally, I thank my publisher, Carl Taylor, and my editor,
Jane McGraw, for all their help.

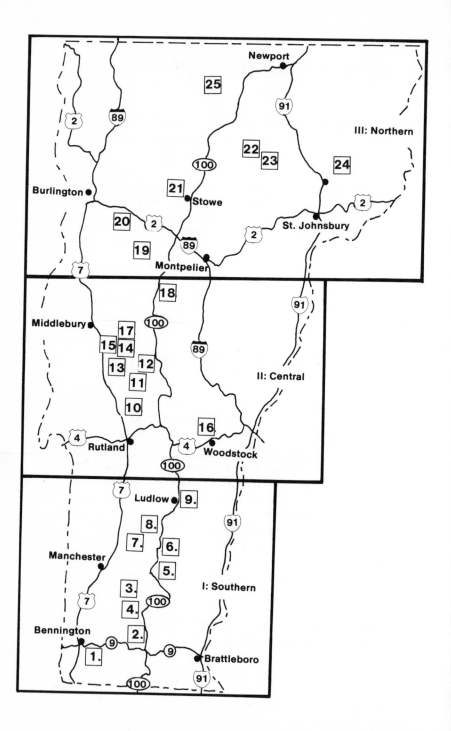

CONTENTS

Snowshoe rabbit tracks

INTRODUCTION

Cross-country skiing imparts to its participants a feeling of freedom, of being "out there" on your own—sensations long gone from our smooth and mechanized downhill ski areas. With cross-country skis on, you can experience nature in areas that you cannot otherwise reach, in the peace and quiet that can only be found in a country winter. At the same time, cross-country skiing requires some thought and responsibility to ensure a fun, safe experience.

Vermont has almost unlimited cross-country ski potential, from well-groomed and marked touring center trails to epic backcountry tours. This book will help you get started if you are a beginner, or will help you sort out the many Vermont options if you are an experienced skier.

Touring centers offer many advantages to skiers, a plowed parking lot being not the least of them. Touring centers track and groom their trails so that you get good skiing on less snow. There is no need to wade through knee-deep drifts to reach the trail, and you do not have to expend the enormous energy it takes to break through new-fallen snow. And don't forget the warm ski lodge where you can thaw out your frosty fingers and toes. For all these services, of course, you are expected to pay a fee, which is usually quite reasonable.

Vermont has some elegant resorts dedicated to cross-country skiing. Restaurants, lodging, and all the extras you would expect at a destination vacation site are offered there. But Vermont also offers another type of touring center: the small, family-run operation. These usually feature somewhat smaller trail systems, but the care given their skiers is no less than what is bestowed by the areas with a higher glitz profile. At the smaller centers, the person renting you your skis and issuing your ski pass might be the owner, and the person teaching the ski classes or grooming the trails is the daughter or son. The smaller areas seem to run at a slightly less frenetic pace, and the staff has more time to get to know you.

Backcountry Skiing and Safety

Backcountry skiing is a low-cost option that offers you the freedom to explore the varied and beautiful Vermont countryside in winter.

An important development for cross-country skiers in Vermont is the newly created Catamount Trail, which, when completed, will run from the Massachusetts state line to Canada. Parts of it are used in this book. The Catamount Trail Association marks and clears parts of the trail every season, runs tours during the winter, and publishes a map and guide to the trail. It also offers a tour that traverses the entire trail at the end of each season. The group starts at the Massachusetts border and skis to Canada. You can make the whole trip or join in for just a day. The group deserves your support. Write to The Catamount Trail Association, Box 897, Burlington, Vermont 05402, for more information.

With the freedom that comes with backcountry skiing comes some added responsibility. There is no ski patrol in the backcountry, thus it is vital that you let someone know where you plan to ski and when you will be back. Your friends should know who to call in case you don't return on time and be able to describe your car (a license number can be useful as well). It is also helpful for them to know what sort of equipment you are carrying, that is, whether or not you are capable of staying out overnight and if you have had first aid and survival training.

Take time to go through a book on winter camping and survival. Knowledge of what kind of trouble you might expect can help you decide what gear to include in your day pack.

One common difficulty on the trail is equipment failure: breaking a ski or pole, losing a binding bail, or having a screw come loose. A small repair kit should include a spare binding, screws and screwdriver, bailing wire, and a roll of duct tape. A spare ski tip is also not a bad idea.

A group of backcountry skiers should consider carrying a change of clothes, one sleeping bag, and a tarp for shelter in case someone gets hurt. If your group is small and this would be too heavy a load, at least carry a space blanket. Always carry a stove or fire starter. Each member should have a headlamp to use if it gets dark while you are skiing back. Although the return trail may be already packed and thus faster, remember that blowing and drifting snow can quickly fill the trail in. And don't let one skier in your party break trail for long periods of time; cold feet will result from pushing fresh snow.

Clothing

Dressing for the weather is of utmost importance in cross-country skiing. It is now possible to buy clothing designed especially for this sport. Gone are the cotton dungarees and sweatshirts that absorb water like a sponge.

Polypropylene, Thermax, and Capilene, the artificial fabrics used in long underwear products, move sweat away from the skin. No matter how hard you may be working, you will feel warm and dry. Polarlite, Polar Plus, and Synchilla are good materials for use in overlayers, because they provide lightweight insulation. Add to that a windbreaking layer, a good hat, and mittens, and you should be dry and warm in most conditions.

Feet get cold if they are not well cared for. Use a liner sock, and cover that with a wool sock. Never use cotton. Make sure your boots are comfortable and not tight. If you add gaiters—leg covers to keep snow out of the tops of your boots—you should be comfortable. If you still have problems, consider overboots—lined covers that fit over your ski boots.

Frostbite and frostnip occur when the surface of the skin freezes. Nip is easy to deal with; usually covering a nipped nose with a warm hand will quickly return blood flow. Frostbite occurs when the tissue freezes more

Central Vermont's hills are excellent places to practice your telemark turns

deeply. The affected area takes on a doughy consis-
tency. Both frostbite and frostnip have the same
cause—cold and usually windy weather. Keeping your
face covered with face masks will protect that area, and
mittens will protect the fingers. You need to watch your
friends for small white patches on noses, cheeks, and
ears. Frostbite is very serious and will require, at the
very least, a visit to the doctor. The higher into the
mountains you go, the colder and more windy it gets,
and the more potential for frostbite and nip there is.

Food and Drink
Food and drink are key parts of your touring kit. And
don't forget that substantial breakfast or lunch before
you go out. You will need that food not only to give you
energy but to keep your body warm. It is important to
carry some high-energy food with you. "Good old raisins
and peanuts," or "GORP," is an excellent and easy energy source. Add crackers or more dried fruit, put it in a
plastic bag, and stick it in your parka pocket for instant
access. The new beltpack water bottle holders are perfect for skiing. They are even insulated. Dehydration can
surprise you in the winter. Although you do not feel as if
you are losing liquid, you are working up a sweat, and
water vapor is exiting your mouth and nose as you
breathe. Not having enough to drink will leave you feeling tired and will take a lot of the fun out of skiing.

Always include a small thermos of hot drink for emer-
gency use. You never know when you might fall in a
brook (which I managed to do last season).

Waxless or Waxed Skis?
I skied most of the tours in this book on waxless skis, so
I didn't have to carry a wax kit or worry about the wax-
of-the-day. Waxless skis are slower though, which can
be a problem if you are skiing with people who are waxing their skis and doing it well. But on those days when

they make a mistake, you will be miles ahead. It makes sense to have both kinds of skis. You can use your waxed skis on days when it is cold and powdery, the easiest waxing conditions, and waxless skis on days when there is warm air and changeable, melting snow. I did use waxable skating skis where the tracks were packed. It is a great new technique and easy to learn, but it does require specialized equipment. Skating with your old touring equipment would be like running a mile in five-pound hiking boots.

If you are skiing on waxable skis, you will need to carry a wax kit and scraper. There are some easy-to-use two-wax systems for wet and dry snow that help keep your load to a minimum. If you add to that a universal klister, you are prepared for any change in conditions. For those using waxless skis, carry a glide wax for added speed and a spray deicer to keep balls of snow from sticking to the bottom of your skis. A scraper can also come in handy for taking icy patches off skis.

Don't try long backcountry tours on equipment you have not yet used. The differences in performance could be surprising or even dangerous. For example, you might find that the skis won't turn well in soft snow or that the waxless surface doesn't work on hard snow.

Enjoying Nature

A book on animal tracks is great fun to have on the trail. A pair of small binoculars will help you enjoy the view, and although there are not a lot of birds around in the winter, they are much easier to watch without the leaves on the trees.

Your Vehicle

Your vehicle needs some special thought. Bring a shovel to dig out a parking spot or to uncover your car if it has been snowing. A bag of sand or kitty litter in the trunk helps you get out of slippery spots, and a tow cable can be a lifesaver for getting a stuck car out of a snowbank. Jumper cables are good protection against a dead battery. Also consider carrying a carburetor deicer like Quick Start. It can get very cold in Vermont, and your starter may need some help turning over the motor. In backcountry areas, be prepared to spend a snowy overnight in the car; keep a warm sleeping bag in your trunk.

Unfortunately, break-ins of cars at trailheads have become a problem in Vermont. Particularly when skiing backcountry trails, remove all valuables from your car or at least hide them in your trunk.

Trail Use Guidelines

Try not to ski alone, even at a ski center. In addition to safety concerns, it is simply more fun to share the experience of skiing with someone else.

It has been somewhat of a tradition to ski with the family dog. Although dogs have a wonderful time, they really trash the tracks. I have also seen a dog badly hurt when it didn't get out of the way of a skier coming downhill. And if that skier had been hurt, the dog owner would have been responsible for all the medical expenses.

If you must walk up or down a hill, don't walk in the ski tracks. The holes you make can be dangerous for other skiers.

Finally, don't trash the wilderness. If you carry it in, carry it out. Use a small bag for garbage.

Trail Descriptions and Maps

Maps in this book are based on the latest available information, but things change every year. Trails get rerouted for various reasons, so get current U.S. Forest

Service (USFS) maps for the backcountry tours and ski area maps for the centers. U.S. Geological Survey (USGS) maps are helpful if you want to know how much elevation you will gain or lose, but in most cases the trails have been cut since the maps were last revised and will not show up on them. They do help you get a general idea of how the surrounding land is shaped. USGS quadrangles for Vermont can be ordered from the National Survey, Topographical Office, Chester, Vermont 05143. To obtain Forest Service maps, contact: Forest Supervisor, Green Mountain National Forest, P.O. Box 519, Rutland, Vermont 05701 (telephone: 802-773-0300 or 802-733-0324).

Two excellent atlases for the state of Vermont will help you find your way to the tours. They are the *Vermont Atlas and Gazetteer,* published by DeLorme Mapping Company, P.O. Box 298, Freeport, Maine 04032; and *The Vermont Road Atlas and Guide,* published by Northern Cartographic, Inc., P.O. Box 133, Burlington, Vermont 05402.

Difficulty Ratings

Novice trails are fairly flat and require the least technique. Intermediate trails will require a strong snowplow stopping technique in a variety of snow conditions. Expert tours have long, strenuous ups and downs with demanding corners; these trails can also be quite steep and narrow.

One of the problems with rating tours is dealing with changing snow conditions. Soft snow is very forgiving but usually slow. A ski tour rated "novice" can be "expert" if the conditions are hard and icy. An easy tour can become a skating rink so slick that no expert would consider it. Part of being a good skier is knowing how snow conditions affect skiing. Don't let your well-meaning friends lead you on tours you don't feel comfortable skiing. You are the best judge of your skiing ability. If you are a beginning skier, try a ski center trail before venturing into the backcountry. The staff may have trail suggestions that will make your trip a success, and a lesson or two for beginners is in order.

Distances

Distances can be used only to estimate how long a tour will take to complete. Snow conditions greatly affect the time required. I have done a backcountry tour of seventeen miles in four hours when the snow was hard and fast. Two days before, however, it had taken me twelve hours to go ten miles, the conditions being soft, deep, and mushy. We might as well have been on snowshoes.

Northern Vermont's patchwork of fields and woods offers scenic and invigorating skiing

Additional Skiing in Vermont

While it presents some of Vermont's best cross-country skiing, a book of this size can only be an introduction to the impressive variety of skiing experiences the state offers. To help you go beyond the tours described in the book, most chapters conclude with sections on other nearby places to ski—both backcountry locations and touring centers.

Personnel at the ski touring centers described in this book will be able to recommend additional trails at their centers suitable to your ability level. Touring center personnel also can often tell you where the best backcountry skiing in the area is. The District Ranger Offices of the Green Mountain National Forest in Manchester (802-362-2307), Middlebury (802-388-4362) and Rochester (802-767-4777), are another source of information on backcountry touring. These offices offer special winter trail maps and can usually provide information about current trail conditions.

Other resources for cross-country skiers include the cross-country skiing map co-published by the Vermont Ski Areas Association and the Vermont Travel Division, which lists all the ski touring centers in the state. It can be obtained from the Vermont Travel Division, 134 State Street, Montpelier, Vermont 05602 (802-828-3236). As mentioned earlier, the Catamount Trail Association (Box 897, Burlington, Vermont 05402) publishes a map of this new Massachusetts-to-Canada trail, which offers many backcountry skiing opportunities. The most comprehensive guide to the state is *Vermont: an Explorer's Guide* (The Countryman Press, P.O. Box 175, Woodstock, Vermont 05091), which provides a brief summary of the cross-country skiing in each region of the state and tells you about the best places to eat and stay wherever you are skiing.

Have fun skiing in Vermont. Remember, however, that things do change—roads close, loggers affect trails, parking lots are not plowed—and be prepared. If you find the trails or access roads closed, please let the publisher know, so that changes can be made in future editions.

Map Legend

Ѧ   **Appalachian Trail**
Ⓟ   **Parking**
   Main Trail
‧ ‧ ‧ ‧   **Side Trail**
▲   **Mountain**
◄   **Direction of Travel**
△   **Campground**
■   **Shelter**
━━ ▪▪▶   **Road**
◀━   **Reverse Direction of Travel**
⇥   **View**
Ⴖ   **Bridge**

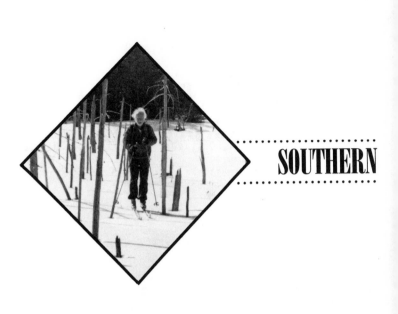

SOUTHERN

PROSPECT MOUNTAIN
SKI TOURING CENTER
Woodford

Difficulty: Novice
Distance: 6 miles
Map: Prospect Mountain Ski Touring Center Map

Prospect Mountain Ski Touring Center is on VT 9, also called the Molly Stark Trail. Molly was the wife of General John Stark of New Hampshire. During the Revolution in August of 1777, General John Burgoyne and the British Army tried to take Bennington, Vermont. Stark and his force of volunteers fought two battles that day, defeating the British in both. It was one of the most important battles of the war.

Access

From Bennington and US 7 in the west, take VT 9 east. The area is on the right about 7.5 miles from the center of town. From the east, take I-91 to exit 2 in Brattleboro, then VT 9 west through Wilmington. The ski area is 12 miles past Wilmington.

The Tour

After getting your ski pass, ski to the right of the downhill area and climb a trail marked with the picture of a cross-country skier. Evergreens surround you on a wide, open trail. A small brook runs under the trail, and you ski sharply to the left up a steep hill. You are now at the top

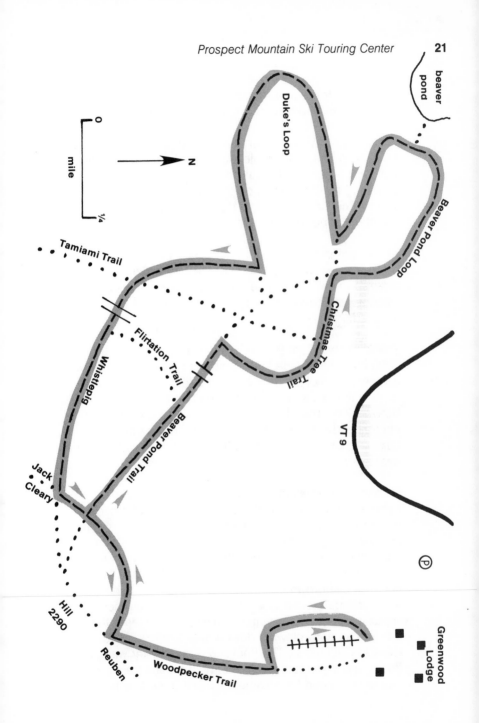

of the rope tow slope. A glance to the left will show you the lodge and parking lot where you started.

Turn right on Woodpecker Trail, which is wide enough to be a road. The trail is typical of those found here. Well built and groomed, the trails show the owners' interest in providing the best skiing on the least amount of snow. The trail continues with little dips and climbs. This trail is not demanding, even for the novice.

At the next intersection, turn right. You will immediately cross a snowmobile trail, one of the Forest Service roads referred to on the ski area trail map. Forest Service regulations prohibit skiing on these trails, so don't be tempted.

You are now on the Beaver Pond Trail. A trail marked 2290 comes in on the left. Ski straight ahead. At the next intersection, trail 2290 leaves to the left. A ski rack and picnic table allow you to rest if you need to. Stay on Beaver Pond Trail. There is a swamp on the left side of the trail and a small rise on the right. The woods are dark with small evergreens, but the trail is so wide that it captures the sun, making things seem open and airy.

Flirtation Trail goes off to the left, but stay on Beaver Pond as it swings right. Some nice views can be had down toward Bennington. Another snowmobile crossing lies ahead with many signs. Ski straight across. At the next intersection, turn right onto Christmas Tree Trail. There is another picnic table off to the side of the trail here. An overgrown trail comes in on the right: Ignore it and continue around to the left. The tracks have been set along the side of the trail, leaving the center of the trail free for snowplowing downhills or skating, if you know the technique. The tracks can be a faster way down, and if you lean into the turns a bit, the tracks will sweep you around the corners. Give it a try. The Tamiami Trail leaves on the left, and another picnic table appears in the open area ahead. Just around the next corner, the Christmas Tree Trail ends, and you are back on Beaver Pond Trail. Ski right.

After some ups and downs, the trail swings around to the left. Climb sharply a short way, then continue to the left. On your right, you will see a trail with no sign but a blue blaze and a number of ski tracks. This is the trail to the beaver pond. You are about halfway through the tour and an easy hour from the lodge.

Take the time to ski down the trail and out onto the pond. The views are great, and you can see a beaver lodge in the pond. These lodges are built with small logs after the beavers have eaten the bark off. Beaver remain active under the ice during the winter. They store their food, branches of small alders and aspens, by sticking them in the mud on the bottom of the pond. When they need food, they swim out, pick a branch out of the mud, and bring it back to the lodge. The lodge has an underwater entrance with a living shelf above water level. The logs of the lodge are packed in with mud, a natural insulator.

Back on the main trail, ski to the next intersection, where there is a trail marked Duke's Loop. Turn right to climb up an easy slope. There is a sign here indicating that the base lodge is to the left, a shorter way back if you need one. Another option is to turn left and repeat the Christmas Tree and Beaver Pond loops for exercise or practice.

Continuing on Duke's Loop, just before the trail goes left there is a sign for an observation point. The short side trail goes up rather steeply. It brings you out over the beaver pond, with views toward the west and Bennington.

On the main trail, keep skiing gradually around to the left past an open cut-over area on the right. At the next intersection, take a right onto Whistlepig. Signs for either trail indicate that you are skiing toward the base lodge.

I skied this trail in a snowstorm and was amazed at how fast conditions can change. My speed slowed considerably because I was pushing against the new snow. The snowfall cut down my visibility and my view of the trail,

Prospect's trails are ideal for skating on skis

and I had difficulty keeping my eyes open on the down-hills. I found that keeping my hand several inches in front of my face kept the snow from blocking my vision.

There are many small evergreens growing under the hardwoods throughout here. At the crossing with Tamiami, stay on Whistlepig. Swing hard to the left and cross the snowmobile trail. Flirtation Trail comes in on the left just after the road crossing. There are many animal signs in this area. Rabbit, deer, and possibly dog or coyote tracks cross and run alongside the trail.

At the next intersection, Jack Cleary comes in on the right. Turn left. Just around the next corner is the intersection with the ski rack and picnic table that you saw on the way out. Trail 2290 goes sharply right and climbs, but you stay on the main trail. Cross the snowmobile trail again and turn left on Woodpecker ahead. The trail rolls mostly downhill back to the top of the rope-tow hill. You can either swing left and downhill to the start or ski down the tow hill. The latter is wide open and an easier ski. The lodge is visible ahead.

Other Places to Ski
The closest other skiing is in Wilmington, Vermont, on VT 9 to the east. The White House Ski Touring Center is located in a lodge on the north side of the road, just east of town. Their extensive trail system is on rolling terrain.

Other options are the Hermitage Cross-Country Ski Area (see Chapter 2) and the Sitzmark Ski Touring Center, both north of Wilmington and just off VT 100. To reach the latter, follow the signs for the Haystack Ski Area and then for the Sitzmark Ski Touring Center. The area has more level terrain, suitable for the novice skier.

THE HERMITAGE
CROSS-COUNTRY SKI AREA
Wilmington

Difficulty: Novice/Intermediate
Distance: 9 miles
Map: The Hermitage Cross-Country Ski Area

The Hermitage Cross-Country Ski Area has been in operation since the early 1970s. The inn is an eighteenth-century farmhouse, famous for having one of the best wine cellars in the area. In the spring, the crew taps 3500 maple trees for syrup. They also raise quail, pheasant, and other more exotic species for sale, in large pens around the building. The ski area is a great destination for a ski week or weekend. The trails are well marked and groomed, and the system is extensive.

Access

From VT 9 east from Bennington or west from Brattleboro, take VT 100 north in Wilmington. Turn left onto Cold Brook Road, after 2.5 miles, toward the Haystack Ski Area. Drive past the downhill ski area; the Hermitage is just up the road on the left.

The Tour

Check in at the ski center and pay your fee. Walk up the hill past the inn to the trail entrance. Ski past the back of the building and go right. A sign indicates that you are at the entrance to all the ski trails. Continue into an evergreen forest with a few birches mixed in. At the first intersection, ski straight ahead on the Ice House Loop

Trail. The trail, which is fairly wide, climbs gradually while turning left and right.

At the next intersection, the Sugar Bush Loop goes left. The trail we are skiing goes right, downhill and over a bridge. Ski down a fairly steep grade to another intersection. Go right. Che's Run goes left. Shortly, turn left and over the bridge on the Cold Brook Trail; Ice House goes straight. A trail enters from the left but is a downhill only run. There are Catamount Trail signs, paw prints on blue diamonds, along this section. After swinging left, the trail climbs gradually on a long uphill section that will test your ski wax job. There are some large beech and ash trees along the trail. Beech trees have a smooth, grey bark, and the younger trees retain their faded, brown leaves through the winter. Ash wood is very dense and strong and used for heavy-duty tool handles.

The trail climbs through a grove of white birches

The Zoom Trail goes off to your left and connects with
Cold Brook at the bottom of the hill. Keep going straight.
Through the trees you can see Haystack Mountain Ski
Area. At the top of the hill, the trail flattens out. The Play-
house Trail comes in on your right, and the Catamount
Trail follows it. Continue on the Cold Brook Trail.

A steep gorge and brook lie to your left. Some big
birches back in the woods do not look especially
healthy. The forest is never static, and the flora is always
adjusting to fluctuations in habitat. The trail is flat for a
bit, then slabs across a hill to the right. The Overcast
Trail goes uphill to your right; continue straight. The trail
crosses a bridge and then climbs steeply. A large dead
tree on your right has been decimated by woodpecker
holes. The holes look as if they were made by the pileated woodpecker, our largest native woodpecker (the
size of a crow). These birds are very shy, and you don't
see them very often. Their holes are easy to identify,
however. They can be ten or more inches long and four
or five inches wide, looking very oblong or oval.

The trail reaches another small bridge. On the left beside the trail is another dead tree full of woodpecker
holes. Here you can see what the birds are after, for the
trunk is riddled with the holes and trails made by insects. The trail climbs less steeply to the right, and you
can see the frosty trees at the top of the ridge on your
left. As the trail starts to level off, a large, lightning-split
yellow birch appears on your right.

At the next intersection, go right. Che's Run goes left,
and the trail you are now on is Winnie's Trail. The trail
goes to the right on a flat section. There are nice views
off to the south and down toward the ski center through
the trees. You are looking in the direction of Wilmington
and, beyond, toward Massachusetts. The trail continues
to roll along, over a bridge and then down a steeper

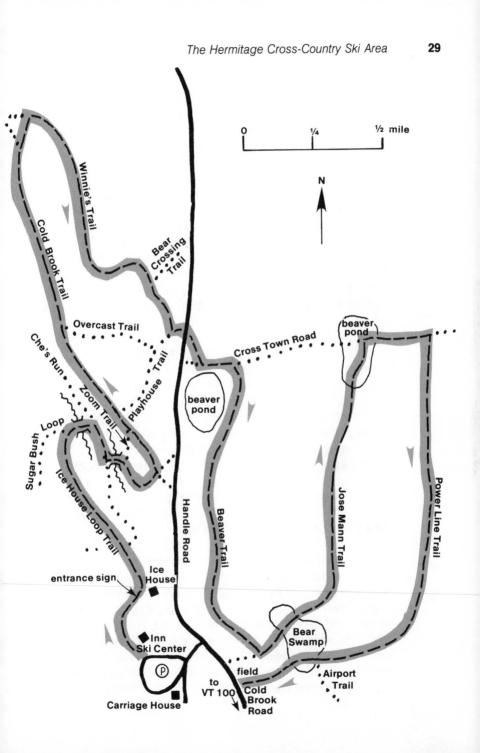

0   ¼   ½ mile

N

Winnie's Trail

Cold Brook Trail

Bear Crossing Trail

Overcast Trail

Cross Town Road

beaver pond

Che's Run

Playhouse Trail

Zoom Trail

beaver pond

Sugar Bush Loop

Ice House Loop Trail

Handle Road

Beaver Trail

Jose Mann Trail

Power Line Trail

entrance sign

Ice House

Inn Ski Center

P

Bear Swamp

field

Airport Trail

Carriage House

to VT 100

Cold Brook Road

section. The path is fairly narrow, so take it slowly. A little-used snowmobile trail comes in on your left partway down. A trail marked "do not enter" goes straight; swing right, over a bridge. The Haystack Ski Area is visible through the trees.

In a stand of large white birches, note where someone has cut a large section off a tree right next to the trail. Tree bark carries nutrients up the tree to feed branches and leaves. Stripping the bark thus robs the tree of nutrients and exposes the underlayers to disease. The trail sweeps left and goes downhill, still in the birches. At the bottom is a sharp lefthand turn, and the section is steep enough to require a strong snowplow. Just above the corner is a spruce tree with several woodpecker holes.

The trail drops quickly to the left. A plywood shed appears on the right, possibly a cover for a well or water pump. Houses are visible to the left. The trail continues to the right and parallels a road. The Bear Crossing Trail goes off to your left; continue to swing right. A brown carriage house comes up on your left. Keep swinging right toward the white house and tennis court, then follow the blue blazes back into the woods. The trail completes an S bend, first left, then right, and parallels a tar road on a powerline. Playhouse Trail goes off right, leading back to the Cold Brook Trail and the lodge. You are now 5 miles from the start of the tour.

Cross the tar road. The trail continues slightly downhill, and you will see Catamount Trail signs again. At the bottom of the hill, just before the pond, take a left onto Cross Town Road. A beaver lodge stands in the middle of the pond on the other side of the road. There is a fairly steep hill ahead, but the trail is wide so staying in control should be easy. At the bottom of the hill, take a right on the Beaver Trail. The Catamount Trail and Cross Town Road continue straight.

The trail climbs gently, passing two large white pines on the right. Continue along a flat section, then ski an easy downhill, gradually turning back to your left. There is a stone wall ahead. The trail swings back up to the left and again is flat. Some huge trees in here probably missed the lumberman's axe because their trunks are split close to the ground. Ski around to the right to the next intersection. A right turn will take you to the field just across the road from the ski center. For a more challenging trail, take a left on the Jose Mann Trail. It is marked most difficult, and the first downhill section demonstrates why: The trail is narrow and has some interesting bumps. Ski to the left. The trail goes through a dense stand of trees, a good place to look for animal tracks. Swing around to the left and down to a beaver pond or swamp. Ski straight across this wet area, go up a hill, and end up back in another section of the swamp. Go across the flat and swing back to the left. The woods are thin here; it has been cut over recently. An open, swampy area lies to the left, and you can just see the top of the Mount Snow Ski Area through the trees.

Ski in and out of several dips. The next intersection is a T with Cross Town Road. Turn right and ski up the hill toward the powerline. Turn right on the Powerline Trail, which follows the powerline over some fairly substantial ups and downs.

The trail swings gradually back toward the right, with Haystack Mountain straight ahead. The Airport Trail enters on your left, another section of the Catamount Trail that comes from the south. The Airport Trail also connects with Sitzmark Ski Center. You can ski over there for lunch in their lodge.

The Power Line Trail crosses a brook. The day I skied this tour, an animal, possibly an otter, had come up the brook on the ice. The tracks were plainly visible in the

snow. Otters move somewhat like an inchworm: The
front feet move out first and the rear feet catch up. The
prints are thus rather square and boxy looking.

Continue up a steep, short hill. There are several houses
on the left. When you reach the field, turn right, following
the top of the field. You can see the lodge ahead. Ski to
the road and walk across the bridge and into the parking lot.

Other Places to Ski

There are two places close by that offer good skiing.
The Sitzmark Ski Touring Center is just down the road,
and, as mentioned in the tour, you can ski over for
lunch. The other place in Wilmington is the White House,
a turn-of-the-century mansion perched on a hill above
Wilmington. Its touring center offers twenty-two groomed
trails traversing rolling terrain and is located just east of
Wilmington on VT 9.

STRATTON POND
West Wardsboro

Difficulty: Intermediate/Expert
Distance: 9 miles
Map: USFS Londonderry SW

This area sits in the midst of the Green Mountain National Forest. The land was once farmland and has since been logged many times, thus providing many nice, wide roads in the area to ski on. The starting point of the tour is a quarter mile beyond the Daniel Webster Memorial Acre, the site of Daniel Webster's famous speech on why only the Whigs could save the Union. There were fifteen thousand people on this spot in July of 1840.

The trail into Stratton Pond is a classic. It starts on wide roads and climbs steeply. There is some flat skiing, but it is a taxing tour with every kind of terrain you can imagine. You need to go with a group of strong, capable skiers.

Access

The mountain road from Arlington to West Wardsboro is closed in the winter. From the west, then, you must travel to VT 100 and West Wardsboro via VT 30 or VT 9. In West Wardsboro, turn west on Kelly Stand Road. After 7 miles you will reach the Daniel Webster Memorial Acre. The parking lot for the trail is at the end of the plowed section of the road, about a quarter mile beyond the Webster Acre.

The Tour

From the parking lot, turn west and ski up over the snowbank. Watch for snowmobile traffic throughout this tour. You should be able to hear them coming and get off the trail well in advance. You will be skiing a section of the Massachusetts-to-Canada Catamount Trail (see Introduction). The trail is marked with small blue diamonds with a cat's paw on it.

Ski uphill gradually along unplowed Kelly Stand Road. After about ⅓ mile, turn right off the road on to the Catamount Trail. The trail is sometimes packed by snowmobiles, which can result in bumps that are tricky to negotiate. The trail swings right, then left, and reaches an open area. Swing up toward the right—a great downhill run on the way back. Ski past a wide spot, probably used for a log dump when this area was last logged.

You can see the top of Stratton Mountain through the trees on the right. Behind and below are Somerset Reservoir and Mount Snow. Large, deformed trees along the trail have been passed over by the loggers. At the next Y, take a left and climb steeply. You will notice that the right branch seems to end in a large, open area below you, probably another log loading area.

At the end of the long climb, the trail flattens and becomes rolling. Watch for snowshoe hare tracks and signs of other small animals in the snow. There are several abrupt dips caused by small streams, so take care. There is a large yellow birch along here; one of the biggest I have ever seen.

The trail becomes steeper and narrower, and the skiing can get tricky if the conditions are fast. A swamp below you on the left is visible down through the trees. The trail goes through a patch of dense spruces. The trail slabs along the hillside, and you can see an old school bus

An open area bordering the trail to Stratton Pond

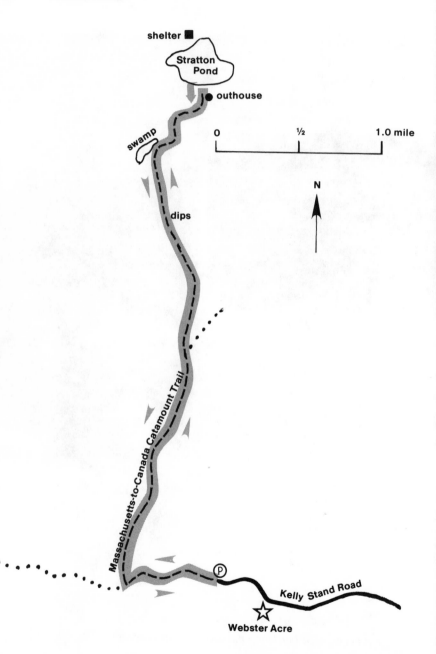

shelter ■

Stratton
Pond

outhouse

0   ½   1.0 mile

N

swamp

dips

Massachusetts-to-Canada Catamount Trail

Ⓟ

Kelly Stand Road

☆
Webster Acre

above you in the woods. The bus was driven here during the 1960s and used as a camp. Ski along the right edge of several swamps.

The trail takes a sharp right and climbs steeply up the hill on your right. After skiing around to the right, you reach the top, and Stratton Pond appears ahead at the bottom of the hill. There is a shelter across the lake, and an outhouse stands by the trail at the top of the hill.

The ski back uses the same 4.5-mile trail. One observation about narrow downhills: They can be attacked with a variety of techniques. One of our party chose to slide down the big hill on his behind; several others took off their skis and walked along the edge of the trail. One person tried to use his poles as a brake by putting them between his legs and sitting on them: He broke both poles. Perhaps the last is not the best technique, but anything is preferable to kissing a pine.

Other Places to Ski

Just down the Kelly Stand Road toward West Wardsboro is an excellent backcountry tour, the Somerset Tour (see Chapter 4). Another challenging backcountry tour is approached from the west end of Kelly Stand Road. From VT 7A in Arlington, follow signs to East Arlington and then to the villages of Kansas and East Kansas. Drive to the end of the plowed section of the road, and park. You can ski into the Lye Brook Wilderness to the north of the road; the skiing potential here is unlimited. You will, however, be skiing on a snowmobile trail; so ski with care.

For maintained trails, the nearby West Dover–Wilmington area offers many opportunities (see Chapter 2). The tourist information booth on VT 100 in West Dover can provide additional information on local skiing opportunities.

SOMERSET RESERVOIR

West Wardsboro

Difficulty: Novice
Distance: 4 miles
Map: USFS Londonderry SW

For the skier new to backcountry Nordic skiing, this tour may be the first one in this book to choose. The great scenery, quality trails, and interesting terrain make a tantalizing mix. The tour is almost entirely flat and gives views of the mountains to the south and east at the end of your outbound leg. One advantage of an in-and-out tour is that your return route is always secure. On a backcountry loop tour, you can be almost back to your car when you hit a brook that is too high to cross and requires that you ski your whole route in reverse.

Even though this tour's difficulty rating is easy, you should still be prepared to spend the night on the trail (see Introduction). Warm clothes for a wet and injured skier are a must. Also include a headlamp for each person so you can continue skiing after dark if you underestimate your speed. Consider equipping your vehicle as well. Back roads are the last to be plowed in a snowstorm, so you may get back to your car only to find yourself spending the night there.

Access

From VT 100 in West Wardsboro, follow signs for the West Wardsboro Store. The road you are on is called Kelly Stand Road, although it does not have a sign. Follow the road about 7 miles to the end of the plowed section. The parking lot is obvious.

The Tour

The Somerset Reservoir is at the headwaters of the Deerfield River. You will be skiing next to one of the feeder streams, known as the East Branch of the Deerfield River, throughout this tour. From the parking lot, ski south. The trail is not marked but should be obvious from use. Ski through an open area first to the left and then around to the right. On the other side of the stream, you can see a large pile of sawdust. There must have been a sawmill here at some point, but all you can see is the sawdust. Small birds flit from branch to branch. You can sometimes see them knocking the seeds off the tops of the dead grasses poking through the snow.

Ski along the side of the brook through a mix of hardwoods and softwoods. The trail swings left away from the river, and then back toward its banks again. A trail leaves on the left. Ignore it, unless you are interested in doing a little cautious exploring, an advantage of backcountry skiing. At a touring center, should you ever venture off a marked trail, the ski patrol comes scampering after you, and that can be really embarrassing.

An open area appears on the right—a dangerous place to ski. The area is covered with ice since it is a floodplain for the stream. After a flood, the surface freezes; when the water retreats, the ice is undermined and will collapse if you ski on it.

At the next dip, there is a strong stream that has no bridge over it. Turn left, ski up the brook, and ski across a beaver dam to the right. Although you can see the trail throughout this operation, keep in mind where you are going. Crossing over the dam is the easiest way to get over the stream.

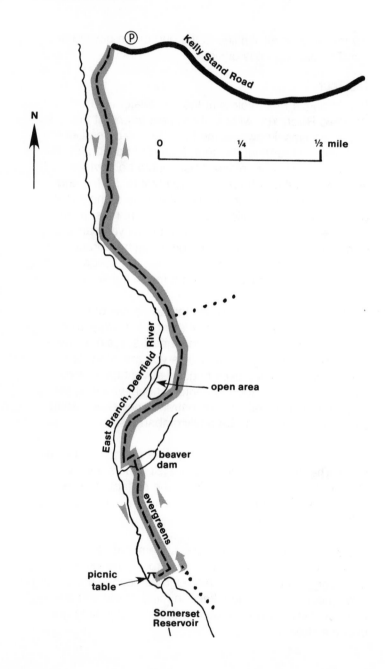

Ski through a dense stand of small evergreens and climb gradually. You are now above the brook, which is on your right. This is one of the few hills on the tour, and it might be stretching it to give it even that status. Ski to the right after the downhill and into a stand of scraggly birches. You then ski back to the stream. After another incline, the trail opens up, and you will get views of Mt. Snow's Northface ski trails. Somerset Reservoir is visible ahead. You can continue along the left bank of the stream, then ski uphill and make a sharp right at a trail intersection. Soon you will get great views to the south and see a picnic table on the right.

When you are ready to return, retrace your path.

Other Places to Ski

For a more challenging backcountry tour, try the Stratton Pond tour, which starts just across the road from this one (see Chapter 3). Another challenging backcountry tour goes into the Lye Brook Wilderness from the west end of the Kelly Stand Road (see Chapter 3 for directions). For maintained trails, the nearby West Dover–Wilmington area offers many opportunities (see Chapter 2). The tourist information booth on VT 100 in West Dover can provide additional information on local skiing opportunities.

5
THE SALMON HOLE
AND DUMPLINGS

Jamaica

Difficulty: Novice
Distance: 7 miles
Map: USFS Londonderry SE and NE

Jamaica, Vermont, is famous for its national-level competition in both canoeing and kayaking. The raging white water of the West River is a test for the best paddlers in the world. In May, usually the first weekend, water is released from the dam at Ball Mountain, just above where our ski tour will end. Jamaica State Park opens, allowing river access, and hundreds of paddlers come from all over the East to test their skills against the river. In winter, the campground closes, the roads remain unplowed, and a frozen quiet settles on the roaring river. There is no better time to explore the area.

Access

Take VT 30 to Jamaica. In town, turn east on Depot Road. A sign to the Jamaica School is on the corner. After you cross the bridge, you will see a small, plowed parking area before the gate to the state park. If there is no room to park here, you will have to park in town, but it is a short walk.

The Tour

Ski around the gate and past the park office on your right. It is very flat skiing. At the first junction, take the left fork and pass by some Adirondack shelters on the left. Keep going, following the road.

Rapids on the West River

At an open area ahead, a road leaves to the right. Ski past the bathroom building, closed this time of year, and travel back into the evergreens ahead. To your left is a big pool in the river. It is called the Salmon Hole, even though more than one hundred years have passed since the salmon came up this river from the ocean. They used to come up the Connecticut River to Brattleboro, where the West River enters. Waste dumped into the river during the 1800s killed off the salmon, and the dams built to produce power closed the river to the returning fish. There are now fish ladders around the remaining dams, and the water is clean enough to support the species. Take time to read the signs about the efforts to bring back the salmon. The river has been stocked with young fish, who will eventually swim to the sea. After several years, they will return to the site of their youth to spawn. If the efforts are successful, eventually the Salmon Hole will no longer be a misnomer.

You can see the campground above you on the right. After a quick right and left, the trail runs along a shelf above the river. A sign indicates that you are on the Railroad Trail and heading for Cobb Brook, Adams Pond, Overlook, and Hamilton Falls. The other side of the river has big rock ledges and white pines rising from the bank. You are skiing on the shadow side of the river and perched precipitously above the water.

Swing slowly to the right and slightly away from the river. There were numbers on the trees. We used numbers like these to indicate where we were to stock salmon for the Department of Environmental Protection in Connecticut rivers, so these numbers might be related to the salmon reintroduction. When we did our stocking, we loaded small salmon into garbage cans lashed inside our canoes and paddled them downriver to the assigned spot, carefully chosen by fish biologists. We dumped them in, and watched them swim away.

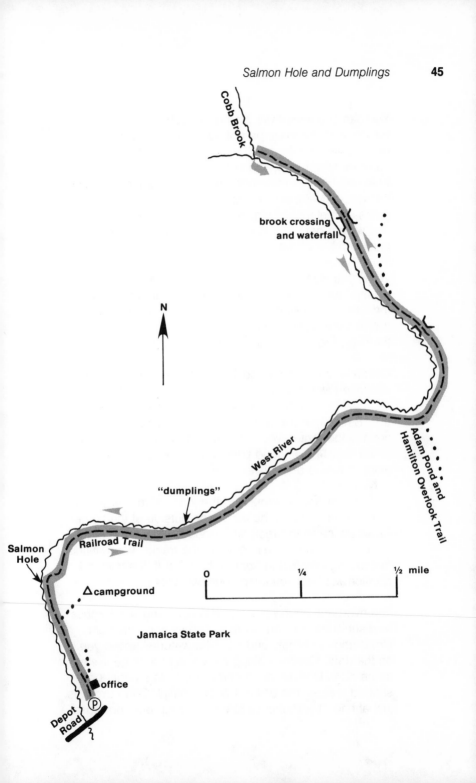

Cobb Brook

brook crossing
and waterfall

N

West River

Adam Pond and
Hamilton Overlook Trail

"dumplings"

Railroad Trail

Salmon
Hole

0   ¼   ½ mile

△ campground

Jamaica State Park

office

Depot
Road

P

You can see some wire strung through the trees along the edge of the road, part of the timing and communications system for the white water race course. If you look carefully at the river, you will see thin cables stretched from one bank to the other. These are used to hang slalom gates over the river. Paddlers must go through the gates, sometimes downstream, sometimes upstream. The winner gets through the course fastest and hits the least number of gate poles.

When you ski back closer to the river, watch for the "dumplings." These are big boulders that partially block the river. Climb slightly, and head back to the right. The trail is once again pinched between the rock ledges and the river. Big icicles hang from the ledges.

Overlook and Adam Pond Trail leaves on the right, but continue toward Cobb Brook. Views of rock ledges and mountaintops on the other side of the river are spectacular. Because the sun doesn't reach in here until afternoon in the winter, you might want to take this tour late in the day. I have found piles of snow and ice in May along this side of the river.

As the river swings around to the left, notice how the ice is forced up onto the banks on the outside of the corner. Cross an ice-filled brook on a good bridge. If there are many sticks and leaves covering the tracks, you will find that sliding one foot in front of the other in the telemark position will help you keep your balance.

The riverbank on the other side is flattening out. Birches now surround you. An old road comes in on the right. Cross another brook, and note the waterfall above you on the right. Continue along the edge of a ledge system to the right. Upriver, on the ridge top, sits a large, ball-shaped ledge—the ball of Ball Mountain? Cobb Brook is just ahead. If you choose to extend your tour and cross

Cobb Brook, be careful, for it is a big stream. The return to your car is via the same route.

Other Places to Ski

From the same parking lot, you can turn right and ski along the river to the south. It's a pleasant route, although the terrain is not as spectacular. Not far away are the two backcountry tours, Stratton Pond and Somerset (Chapters 3 and 4), off the Kelly Stand Road west of West Wardsboro. Also within easy reach is the Peru-Londonderry area, which offers good backcountry and touring center skiing (see Chapters 6–8).

6 VIKING SKI TOURING CENTRE

Londonderry

Difficulty: Intermediate
Distance: 8 miles
Map: Viking Ski Touring Center

Viking is one of the longest lasting ski touring centers in Vermont. Established in the early 1970s, this well-run operation has served thousands of skiers. The trails are impeccably groomed, and there is a good restaurant, a ski shop, and certified instruction. You couldn't ask for a better ski experience.

Access

From the east, take VT 103 west off I-91 at Rockingham (exit 6). In Chester follow VT 11 west. To reach the ski area entrance, turn right on Little Pond Road about 14 miles from Chester. The turn is well marked.

From the west, take VT 11 east out of Manchester, Vermont. Little Pond Road is about .8 mile east of Londonderry.

The Tour

The tour traverses both ski center property and private land that the area has used for years, having established good relations with the local landowners. The trails are carefully cut and groomed throughout the system.

After paying the fee at the lodge, go uphill toward the rental building. Ski to the right in the field and head toward the woods. Sugarbush Run leaves to the right from the upper corner of the field. You are also following arrows to Cobble Hill. The trail is double tracked.

Wire to light the trail system runs above your head. A house appears at the bottom of a short, steep downhill, and the trail swings left, paralleling the road. At the next intersection, bear right and cross the road. You are now on the Boynton Run. There are some houses on the right, for this is part of Viking's private land system. The trail continues through a field with evergreens. Differing snow conditions might be experienced here: sticky in the open and icy under the trees in warm weather. The trees here, balsam fir, send forth their characteristic fragrance.

A new cut-off trail goes off to the right and uphill. Stay on Boynton. I skied this tour on a warm day after a wet snowfall. A low fog hugged the ground, and bright sunlight filtered down through the trees, an unusual sight.

After climbing gradually, you reach Roundabout Trail. Take it sharply uphill and to the right. A huge broken tree lies on the left. It is amazing how much bigger trees seem when they are lying on the ground. Ski through a pine grove on a flat trail. The trail follows the natural contours of the hill.

Climb sharply left. The cut-off trail from the Boynton Run enters on the right.

Ski across a flat spot. You will notice large, snowy mounds along both sides of the trail. These are large stone walls. Beaver Pond Trail leaves to the right in an overgrown pasture; take it.

You will see the beaver pond, an open area with dead
trees, below you on the left. At the bottom of a small hill,
you ski over a bridge that crosses the outlet of the pond.
You then climb again. Notice the shaggy yellow birches
along the trail.

The trail meets Ridge Run, which goes straight ahead. It
is one-way and not accessible from this end. Instead,
ski sharply left and through an opening in the stone wall.
Cobble Hill Trail is the next intersection; continue
straight on the Beaver Pond Trail. Cobble Hill Trail is the
longest loop trail at Viking. Don't be tempted to start it
unless you have allowed plenty of time. The staff at the
ski shop can tell you how long it will take.

The beaver pond is again visible on your left, downhill.
There are lots of quick dips along the trail. If you are
having trouble with stability, try putting your skis in a telemark position as you pass through a dip: one foot for-
ward and one foot back, with your knees bent. This
position adds a lot of stability.

The downhill ski trails at Magic Mountain are visible over
the pond. Ski uphill and away from the pond. Roundabout Trail appears in front of you. Go right, up the hill.
You can hear both the local downhill ski areas from
here. The Chute Trail goes off to the left and is marked
as most difficult. Stay on Roundabout.

Ski downhill gradually, although it can be fast if the surface is hard. The bottom is wide and flat, but you still
have to make it around a corner to the left. Stay in control. After the turn, the next few minutes of skiing are
great for double-poling: a slight downhill with nice
tracks. After a short uphill, you reach a T intersection
with Boynton Run. Go right and downhill. You can see
Boynton Road below and parallel to the trail.

Stop where there are danger signs. Cross the road, ski

Passing a beaver pond

a few yards, and at the first intersection go straight onto Pine's Run. There is a farmhouse visible on the left. After passing Cobble Hill Trail on your right, ski left and over a driveway. A trail soon leaves to the right, and after a short distance another trail enters from the left. Ski through a pine grove, following signs for the touring center (a little more than 3 miles away). Climb steeply out of the pine grove and turn left. The knob rising to your right is covered with small birches. At the next intersection, a Y, stay right on Pine's Run. Ski left on Viking at the next intersection and soon cross Sugarbush Run. The area is covered with evergreens. It is always surprising how cold it is in the shade. Ski left onto Norseman and follow it, climbing slightly to the center.

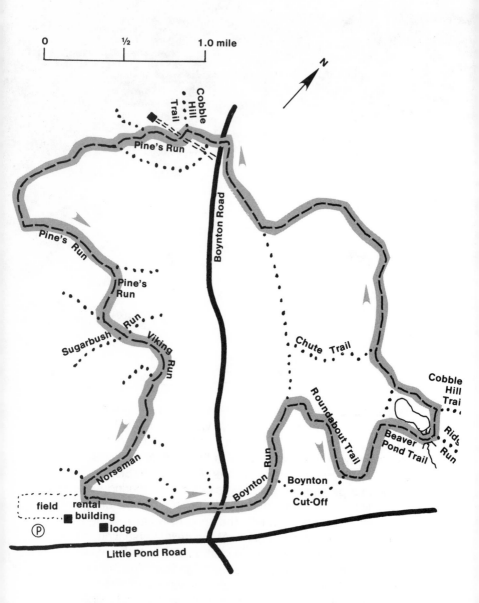

0   ½   1.0 mile

N

Cobble Hill Trail

Pine's Run

Pine's Run

Pine's Run

Boynton Road

Sugarbush Run

Viking Run

Chute Trail

Cobble Hill Trail

Roundabout Trail

Beaver Pond Trail

Ridge Run

Norseman

Boynton Run

Boynton Cut-Off

field   rental building   lodge

Ⓟ

Little Pond Road

Other Places to Ski

Wild Wings Ski Touring Center, located 2.5 miles north of Peru, offers some twelve miles of skiing, much of it geared to the novice skier (see Chapter 7). There is also an extensive public trail system linked to the Wild Wings and Viking trail systems. You can ski to the village of Weston for lunch. The District Ranger Office of the Green Mountain National Forest in Manchester (802-362-2307) may be able to suggest backcountry tours in nearby areas of the GMNF.

7 WILD WINGS SKI TOURING CENTER
Peru

Difficulty: Novice
Distance: 2.5 miles
Map: Wild Wings Ski Touring Center Map

The Wild Wings Ski Center is a family-run operation.
Angus and Jean Black opened the center in 1974. They
have now passed the daily operations on to their son
Chuck and his wife, although Angus says he is still in
charge of the parking lot. The area services the local
communities as a recreational resource. The local
school kids take part in a Bill Koch Ski League program,
and on weekday afternoons there are many young skiers
on the trails. The area offers a nice mix of terrain, great
for any level skier. The tour I describe here is an easy
one, great for beginners.

Access

From VT 11, turn north in the town of Peru, following
signs to Hapgood Pond. Take the third left, about 1 mile
from the center of Peru. Then take the fourth left. After
Peru, there are signs at the intersections. Don't forget to
pay the trail fee before you set out.

The Tour

Across the road from the lodge, the Woodcock Trail
starts by heading left along the edge of a grove of white
pine. Go straight at the first intersection, skiing next to
the entrance road. Ski through a quick down and up.
When skiing across a slope, remember to use the edges

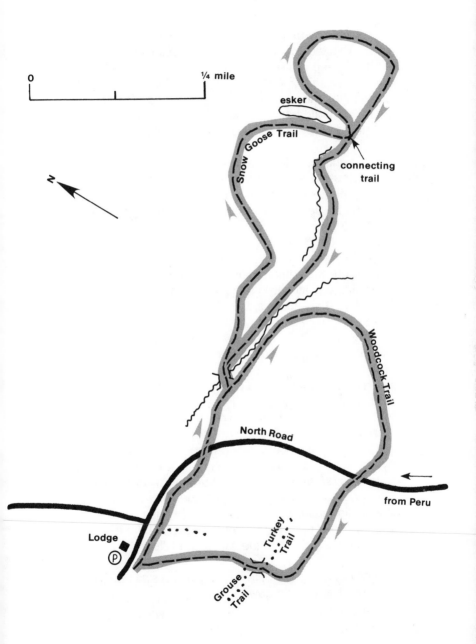

0   ¼ mile

N

esker

Snow Goose Trail

connecting trail

Woodcock Trail

North Road

from Peru

Turkey Trail

Grouse Trail

Lodge
Ⓟ

of your skis by pushing your knees toward the uphill slope. This technique keeps you from sliding sideways. A short, steep dip brings you out to the road; the trail continues straight across it. Take off your skis and walk across the road, even if it is snow covered. The gravel wears the bottom of your skis, and any salt on the road will stick to the bottoms and slow your glide.

Swing right, following a brook on your left. Turn left on Snow Goose Trail and ski to the bridge. In low snow years, bridges have been known to eat ski poles: If you stick the tip between the slats and ski away, the pole tip will break off.

Cross the bridge and go straight on the Snow Goose Trail. There are some beautiful yellow-white bracket fungi shaped like shells attached to a tree on the left side of the trail, and a stand of black spruces lies ahead. It looks as if a wind storm knocked over a large number of trees. Spruces have very shallow root systems that don't provide support.

Ski through a quick down and up to the right. A nice field on the left through the trees sports a house at the top. A swampy area with a pine- and birch-covered knoll appears on the left. Swing right around the bottom of a glacial esker, a smooth, round-topped hill of gravel left by the last ice age. Ahead is an optional connection between the out and back loops; but the complete loop is easy and not long. The trail swings left just beyond the intersection. Large white and yellow birches line the trail. The trail goes up steeply over the esker. There is a brook on the right, and the skiing is a little more difficult.

A sunny open spot on the left contains a swamp. Climb a small hill and glide down to a flat section before the bridge. You can ski the same loop again if you aren't tired.

To continue, cross the bridge and turn left on Woodcock. Ski uphill, and travel down along the edge of the
hill. There is a small swamp on the left. Ski around the
edge of the swamp to a brook on your left.

Gradually swing to the right past an old cellar hole.
There is an overgrown field ahead. Ski left back to the
road and go straight across it. The trail goes up to the
right over a small hill through a grove of good-sized
white pines. Another trail, the Turkey Trail, enters from
the right. Ski uphill and down over a bridge. Another
quick uphill followed by a short downhill follows. Grouse
Trail enters on your left. Swing toward the left on an old
road. The ski center is visible ahead.

Other Places to Ski

For more challenging skiing at Wild Wings, you might try
the three-mile loop on the Blue Jay Trail. The major por-
tion of the Blue Jay Trail can be combined with the even
more challenging and "primitive" Chickadee Trail for an
invigorating four-and-one-half-mile loop. Other good
skiing in the area includes the Viking Touring Center
(see Chapter 6) and the Mount Tabor backcountry tour
(see Chapter 8). The District Ranger Office of the Green
Mountain National Forest in Manchester (802-362-2307)
may be able to provide information on other tours in
nearby areas of the GMNF.

MT. TABOR ROAD

Peru

Difficulty:	Intermediate
Distance:	6 miles
Map:	USFS Wallingford SE and SW

The Mt. Tabor Road goes from Landgrove to Danby but is open to traffic only in the summertime. During the winter it is not plowed, so the Forest Service uses it for a variety of recreational sports. You will be sharing part of this tour with snowmobilers and snowshoers. A section of the tour is on a trail maintained by the West River Outing Club. All the organizations that cut trails in Vermont are volunteer. Join one and help keep our ski trails open. It's enjoyable to spend a day or two helping a group of like-minded individuals move or cut some brush. You might even meet some people you would enjoy skiing with.

Access

From VT 11, turn north in the village of Peru, initially following signs to Hapgood Pond. Stay on the main road for 4.5 miles until you reach a four-way intersection by the Landgrove town hall. Turn left. After passing the Village Inn on your right, take the first left, .7 mile from the town hall. Cross a brook and take the next right onto Forest Road 10. Parking is just ahead. Please parallel park on the right side of the road, avoiding the plowed turnaround area. The turnaround is to give drivers room to maneuver their snowmobile trailers.

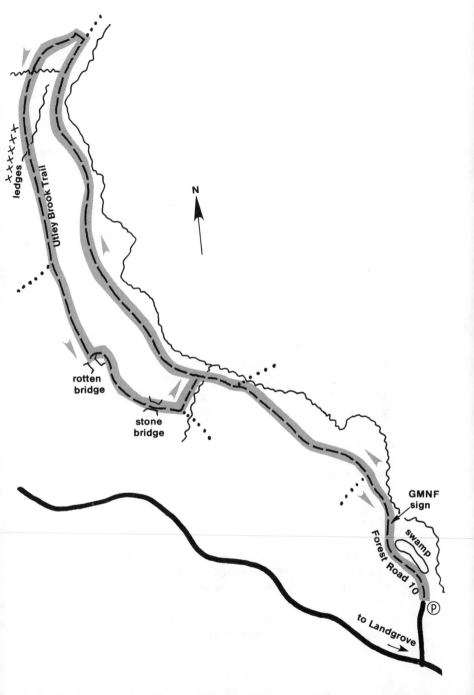

ledges

Utley Brook Trail

N

rotten
bridge

stone
bridge

GMNF
sign

swamp

Forest Road 70

to Landgrove

The Tour

Check the various signs on the bulletin board. They point out any changes in the trails and offer suggestions for trouble-free skiing. There are maps available at the U.S. Forest Service District Ranger Office on VT 11/30 just east of the Manchester exit from US 7. Ski onto the road over the plowed snowbank. The road swings gradually left and right. It is wide and well packed. A swamp is visible beside the road.

This section is what I have always referred to as a thinker's trail. Since it is flat, you needn't pay constant attention to your skiing. Your mind is free to wander, or you can watch for birds in the trees and for animal tracks. The trail part of this tour is very technical and will require you to pay attention.

Around the next corner you will find the Green Mountain National Forest sign. Shortly, a trail leaves on your left. If you look ahead and above you, the ridge line is visible. There are many broken-off evergreens here, snapped off just below the top. They may have been snapped by wind or heavy snow or ice. Some small beech trees, long and thin, stand with the leaves still attached.

Climb gradually and across a small brook. A large brook runs on your right. Keep climbing steadily. There are many yellow birches through this section. When the sun hits them just right, they cast a yellow light on everything, a light, golden glow. The bark of these trees looks shaggy, even on the smallest branches.

Ski right onto a flat section. A road goes across the river to the right, and there is a cutover area on the left. The big brook was dammed by ice when I was here: Large chunks had floated downstream and jammed. Often the water backs up and floods a trail or road. Although it usually happens during the spring melt, it can happen

Forest Service signboards provide important information at trailheads in the Green Mountain National Forest

any time there is extended warm weather. The yellow birches have now switched to the left and evergreens are on the right.

There are ridge views uphill. Another trail leaves left; this is the trail on which you will return. Keep straight, and cross another small brook; notice the large hardwoods on your left as the road sweeps left. I heard a pileated woodpecker call here; it sounds like a very loud blue jay. Several trees are riddled with woodpecker holes. The blue sky against the white birches and dark fir trees makes the colors snap into focus. The contrast almost hurts your eyes.

About 3 miles from the starting point, turn onto the Utley Brook Trail. It is a sharp left. Ski into a sharp dip and into an open area. Blue blazes mark this trail. Ski to the center of an open area and turn sharply left. There is a steep hill ahead. After flattening out, the trail sweeps downhill to the right along the edge of a brook. Cross the brook and climb the hill. There are some big birches through here. Ahead of you is a blue blaze on a large evergreen tree. The hole in the tree indicates that the woodpeckers have taken some interest in it, although it still looks healthy and sound. In the open, cut-over section ahead, take a sharp right and climb toward the trees. The trail continues into the woods and slightly to the left. There are some massive ledges above you on the right. Cross a stream and follow it left. You can see where the brook gets its start under the ledges above you.

The tour starts on a wide road

The ledge system is on your right. Continue climbing. At the top, the trail winds right through hardwoods. This sunny, southeast-facing slope may account for the lack of evergreens. At a Y intersection, turn left and head down to the stream below. The trail swings to the right. Ski down steeply at first, then gradually. Watch carefully for the blue blazes; they are hard to see through here. When you reach the brook, ski along its left edge. Avoid the rotten, untrustworthy old bridge. I inadvertently chose this spot to take a little swim—right off the bridge, through the ice, and into the brook. Luckily it was a warm day, and the water was only a couple of feet deep. You never know what's going to happen when you set out on a backcountry ski tour.

The roadbed is visible, but for awhile you ski above it. Swing down and into an indentation ahead. On the left, a careful inspection will reveal a beech tree with many bear claw marks on it. Animals, especially bears, climb up to get the beech nuts in the late summer and fall. After skiing down a sharp downhill and crossing a stone bridge, you reach a point where the main trail crosses another brook and climbs very steeply. A road leaves on the left just before the climb. Turn left on that road and follow the brook. The road you skied up on is less than ¼ mile away, reachable with an easy downhill ski. Turn right when you reach the road. You are less than a half hour away from the parking lot.

Other Places to Ski

For good touring center skiing, try the nearby Wild Wings and Viking touring centers (see Chapters 6 and 7). Both centers are linked to a public trail system, extending as far as Weston. The District Ranger Office of the Green Mountain National Forest in Manchester (802-362-2307) may be able to provide current information on other backcountry tours in nearby areas of the GMNF.

FOX RUN NORDIC CENTER

Ludlow

Difficulty: Novice/Intermediate
Distance: 3.3 miles
Map: Fox Run Nordic Center

The town of Ludlow thrived in the late nineteenth century on the manufacture of shoddy, a material made from recycled wool. More recently the town was sustained by a General Electric aircraft engine parts plant. The town suffered economic doldrums after the 1977 closure of the General Electric plant, but today it is again a busy place. As well as servicing the local population, the Fox Run Nordic Center accommodates the tourists and skiers who come to use the downhill area at Okemo. The downhill ski area is right on the edge of town, providing a backdrop for the cross-country skiing at Fox Run.

Access

From Rutland, take VT 103 from US 7 south of Rutland. The center is just north of Ludlow on the left. If you are coming northbound on I-91 take VT 103 at Rockingham (exit 6) and go through Chester to Ludlow. The center is less than a mile north of town on the right. For those southbound on I-91, get off at exit 8 and take VT 131 west to VT 103. Turn right on VT 103 and follow it to Ludlow.

The Tour

After paying the trail fee, ski out onto the golf course and turn left at the first opportunity. Go down a slight

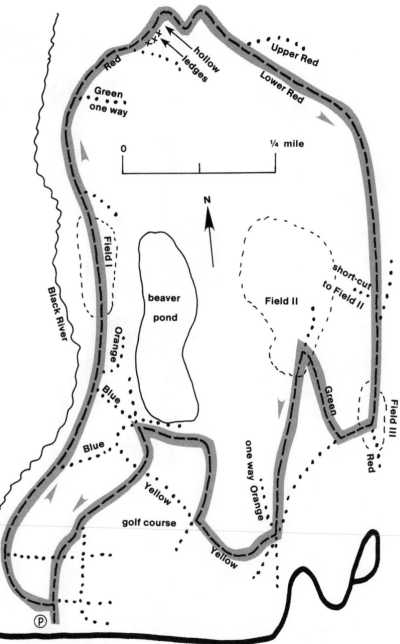

Switchback trails make the climbing easier

hill. Ski into the woods and, at the first intersection, go left on the Orange, Green, and Red trails. Caution signs warn of a downhill ahead, and the Blue Trail leaves our trail to the right. Continue on the Orange, Green, and Red trails. Keep going downhill to the river. The river is the Black, which produces occasional trophy-sized trout for local fishermen and has had some major floods. Keep skiing along the river, looking for signs of animals. The most common river animals are muskrat, beaver, mink and otter. The Orange and Blue trails leave to the right. You follow the Red and Green trails to field number one.

You can hear the sounds of rapidly flowing water in the background. Ski into the pines and spruces, and soon you will see the rapids and riffles you heard. Cross a number of brooks along the hillside.

Climb steeply on the Red Trail. The Green Trail leaves to the right, a difficult downhill coming from the opposite direction. A short distance ahead, another trail leaves on the right. You ski through a little hollow, then swing around to the right below some ledges.

Switchback trails across the slope make climbing easier and prevent the trail from washing away in the spring and summer rains. The large spruces on the left provide shelter for birds. I flushed a partridge from some lower branches. During a snowy winter, snow slides are a possibility on the steep slopes on your left. There are regularly small avalanches on the steep slopes of the Proctor Gulf just south of Ludlow on VT 103.

When you reach the top of the steep section, you will get a good view of the downhill ski area on your right. When I was here last, a small, bounding animal, probably a fox or coyote, had been through here. The tracks looked as if someone had bounced a ball down the hill. There are some caution signs on a downhill ahead. A ledge, with patches of ice glistening, is visible above the trail. The Upper Red Trail goes up to the left, but stay on the Lower Trail. You ski through a low swampy area, where there is a sparkling, gravel-bottomed brook. The trail rolls mostly downhill and then up to field three. From the field, ski down the Green Trail. The trail might have been an old road, with large maples lining its sides. A large tree on the left has been split by lightning at the top.

At the next intersection, take the Green Trail right toward field two. Turn left at the field by a big yellow birch. There is a nice view toward the ski area through a small notch ahead. Go through the notch and down on a wide trail with big trees along the side. Sharp thorns on bare stalks indicate a berry patch on the side of the trail.

The ski complex is visible below, and you can easily see all the trail connections across the open area ahead. But I found the following combination to be interesting. At the next intersection, take the first available trail to the right (except for the one-way Orange trail, which comes in on the near right). Watch the sharp right corner with a section of fence right on the curve! At the next intersection, turn right again and swing away from the complex onto a lane lined with spruces and maples. At the next trail junction, swing sharply back to the left and ski straight toward the ski lodge.

Other Places to Ski

For those preferring groomed trails, the nearest skiing to the north is the Mountain Meadows Ski Touring Center, one of Vermont's oldest touring centers, just off US 4 near Killington. The center offers a well-groomed, twenty-five-mile trail system through high, rolling terrain, as well as a pleasant, hospitable lodge to stay in. Back-country skiing is available on the unplowed roads and snowmobile trails of the Calvin Coolidge State Forest on VT 100A, twelve miles north of Ludlow. Ski with care, because there are many snowmobiles on the trails.

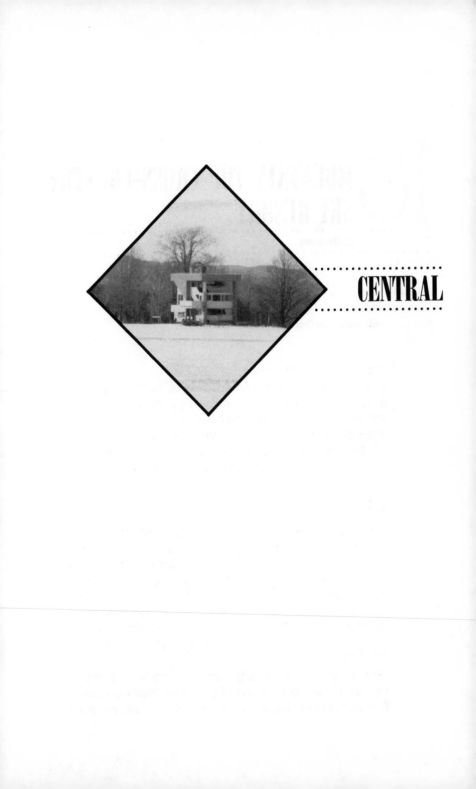

CENTRAL

10 MOUNTAIN TOP CROSS-COUNTRY SKI RESORT

Chittenden

Difficulty: Intermediate/Expert
Distance: 8 miles
Map: Mountain Top Cross-Country Ski Resort Map

The drive up to Mountain Top will help you understand why this area has been so successful, for the snow gets deeper around every corner. Even so, the owners have not left snow to chance and have put in a large snow-making operation. As long as the weather is cold, folks will be skiing here. But the real draw for cross-country skiers is the extensive trail system and the super grooming.

Access

Less than a mile north of Rutland, turn east off US 7 onto an unnumbered paved road, heading toward East Pittsford and Chittendon. Follow the signs to Chittenden, which you will reach in 5.6 miles. At Chittenden, cross the river and turn right up the hill. At each intersection there are signs to Mountain Top. The access road to the resort is on the left 2 miles north of Chittenden.

The Tour

Take a right out of the lodge after paying the trail fee. You will be skiing on a wide trail called Interfield Lower. This section is in the snowmaking system, and you can

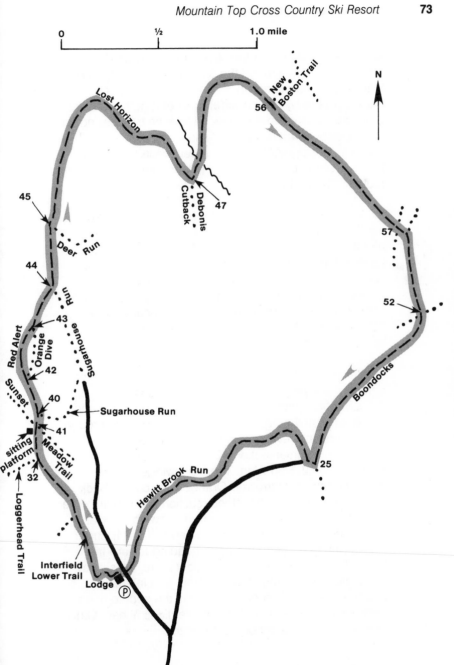

see the pipe along the trail. Continue uphill gradually, making your way around the snowmaking pond. Snowmaking guns are lined up on one side of the pond. Snow is made by mixing air and water together under pressure. The outside air needs to be below freezing for successful snowmaking. The "snow" is actually small ice crystals. Keep going uphill on a very wide trail. At the first intersection, of Upper and Lower Interfield, take the route to the right and uphill.

Ski along the field. It climbs steeply, flattening out on top. To your right are views of the Chittenden Reservoir and the main ridge of the Green Mountains. Ski past the Loggerhead Trail at intersection 32. At the top of the field is a sitting platform where you can rest and look at the view. At intersection 41, ski down Sugarhouse Run Trail, number 14. Sunset goes left and Meadow goes right. Continue for a short distance through black spruces and birches.

At intersection 40, Sugar House Run goes down to the right to a warming hut. Stay on Red Alert, number 12. You climb fairly steeply, with softwoods on the left and hardwoods on the right. Actually, you are skiing through old pastureland, evidenced by the small trees and old stone walls. At intersection 42, Orange Dive goes right. Stay on trail 12, Red Alert. The trail swings right and gets steeper and narrower. Orange Dive comes back into the trail very steeply at intersection 43. You are on a steep trail. Use your snowplow turn to swing back and forth within the packed track. At intersection 44, Sugar House Run goes off to the right, heading toward the lodge. From here, the lodge is about 20 minutes away via Sugar House Run, Meadow Trail, and Interfield Lower; if you are tired or cold, this is the spot to head back, as there are some "expert" sections ahead. Otherwise, continue straight on Lost Horizon.

An open area with small trees and the remains of an old logging operation is visible on the left. A snowmobile trail touches the ski trail. At intersection 45, continue on Lost Horizon. At intersection 46, Deer Run leaves our tour to the right. There is a great skating track through here among big maples and birches. You can see the

Trails at the start of the Mountain Top system are wide and easy

Green Mountain ridge through the trees on the right if
you can slow down long enough to enjoy it.

There is a sign for the Green Mountain National Forest
on a downhill section. Here the government mandate on
multi-use of the National Forest system has been put
into visible action; the mandate calls for recreational use
as well as the harvesting of forest products. The trail becomes a roller coaster track through here. Stay on Lost
Horizon at intersection 47 as it flattens out, crosses a
brook, and then climbs steeply around a small hill. A wet
swampy area and brook are ahead. Look for the large
tracks of a split-hoofed animal through the next several
miles. The largest eastern mammal, the moose, is returning to Vermont, and I saw moose tracks along this trail.

The New Boston Trail goes to the left; ski straight on
Lost Horizon. This section is great for practicing the
marathon skating technique: Keep one foot in the track
and use the other to push yourself along. It is a very fast
technique. A snowmobile trail crosses our trail in a small
open area. Ahead is an intersection with a major snowmobile trail. The New Boston Trail then goes off to the
left, and you keep right, paralleling the snowmobile trail.

At the next major intersection, number 52, a trail that is
open to snowmobiles goes off to the left, circling the
lake. You start swinging back toward the center on
Boondocks. You can see where the lodge is located. Ski
back into white pines, where there is a caution sign.
Snow conditions are apt to be faster under the pines,
but a strong snowplow will slow you down. After about
¾ of a mile, you ski left through a cutover area to an intersection. Turn right on Hewitt Brook Run.

Now you must pay for all the prior downhill runs. Ski
over a large bridge and out of the National Forest. Take
trail number 26, which comes down on your left, all the

way to the lodge. Keep skiing uphill, noticing how the trail is constructed. A wide drainage ditch on the side of the trail is built to keep the dirt from washing away in the spring thaw. The houses you see are part of a community planned to take advantage of the ski trails. The trails pass between the houses, giving the owners easy access to the system. The ski shop and lodge are visible ahead.

Other Places to Ski

From Mountain Top, it is not far to the Mountain Meadows Ski Touring Center's twenty-five miles of trails through rolling, high terrain. Mountain Meadows is just off US 4 near Killington. The easiest way to get there from Mountain Top is to follow the paved road from Chittenden to Mendon, where you turn left (east) on US 4. The trails of Blueberry Hill and Churchill House are also not far away (see Chapter 13).

11 CHITTENDEN BROOK TRAIL

Difficulty: Intermediate (with short Expert section)
Distance: 5.5 miles
Map: USFS Rochester Ranger District Chittenden Brook
Recreation Area Map (normally available at trailhead)

This tour climbs beside a beautiful brook that provides visual interest. At the top of the tour, after a very steep section, you get a great downhill run back to your car. The tour requires good speed-control skills. A section of the trial is called "for experts only" by the Forest Service. I think that being an expert means not only skiing well but also knowing when to take your skis off and walk or when to sidestep a section. When I skied this tour, I sidestepped two hills. The thrill of the run is not worth the pain of an abrupt encounter with a large tree.

The tour is on property belonging to the U.S. Forest Service, and here you can see how their multi-use management plan works. Timber is being cut off the access road, a campground is being maintained at the end of the road, and we are skiing on old logging roads that are used for hiking in the summer.

Access

From the VT 100 and VT 73 intersection near Rochester, take VT 73 west toward Brandon 4.5 miles. The Chittenden Brook Recreation Area is on the left (south) side of VT 73. Coming from Brandon, the trailhead is 12.5 miles down VT 73 on the east side of Brandon Gap. The parking lot is to the right from this direction.

The Tour

This tour begins on Forest Service Road 45, a wide road that leads to a campground in the summer. You climb next to a large brook on the left. After crossing a small stream, the brook and trail swing back to the left in dark evergreens. Ski up to a bridge and over the brook.

The water in the brook is amazingly clear. The White River that this brook feeds is also noted for its clear water. You can see to the bottom of very deep pools. A large glacial erratic, a big boulder, lies on your right as the trail crosses another stream. The main brook is still on the right. When I was there, it had flooded, leaving large, mushroomy mounds of milk-white ice on its banks.

At intersection 2 ahead, take the lower, right option along the brook. It is a narrow passage. The trail turns sharply left, and the banks rise on both sides so that you feel as if you're in a ditch. The brook is pretty, with little falls and deep pools. The last time I was here an ice fall on the left side of the trail had created a cave. It takes a long time for such ice to melt off in the spring. The trail climbs steeply for a bit.

Cross the brook on a major bridge with handrails. After another short climb, the trail flattens out. Another bridge appears ahead. The trees here are very big; it has obviously been a long time since any cutting has been done. Just beyond the bridge on the left is a large tree with a big split in the trunk. You can actually see through the hole in the tree. It is amazing that it can still be strong and healthy.

Climb up and away from the brook to the right. The last time I was there, there were some large ice bulges,

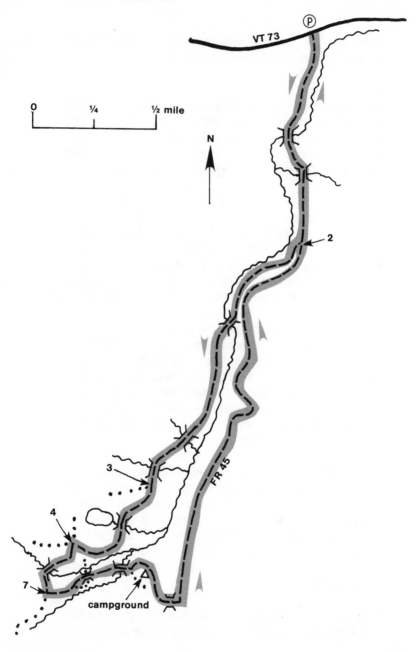

caused by seepage from the ground, on the other side of the brook. After crossing another bridge, swing hard to the right. Swing back to the left and over a bridge. The trail is washed out ahead, but the blue blazes will help you keep on track. If they have re-routed the trail around the washed-out section, the blazes will also help you find your way.

At intersection 3, a little less than 2 miles from the trail-head, take a left and climb gradually. The terrain is more rolling through here. Some big trees are downed along the trail. Ski back to the right and over another bridge. A beaver pond is now above you. Ski around its lower edge and then back up to the right. It is obviously an old pond, with no sign of current activity. Climb steeply again, and at the next intersection, number 4, take a left. The sign indicates you are 2.3 miles from VT 73 and 1.7 from Forest Road 45.

Ski toward the campground, soon coming to another bridge. Take the left at the next intersection, number 7, marked for experts only. It appears to be a path through the woods rather than the wide trail you have been on. (If you wish to keep this an intermediate tour, you may want to turn around at this point and retraice your route.) There are blue blazes visible. After turning left, you swing back to the right and start down a very steep hill. I sidestepped this section. At the next intersection, take a left. Ski down to the brook and over it on a bridge. After the bridge, turn left. The blazes disappear. Continue along the path of least resistance—on the very edge of the brook—and after a short distance, the blazes are visible again. Ski over a bridge. There is a sign here saying that the trail was built by the Ripton Job Corps Center in 1967. Turn left to the campground.

Turn left at the road and ski past outhouses and over-turned picnic tables. The campground looks as if it

An ice fall formed by melting snow towers over the trail

would merit a summer visit. At the next intersection, cross a bridge, turn sharply left, on unplowed Forest Road 45, and climb up a gradual grade. From the top, you get a great ride back to the road and parking lot.

Other Places to Ski

For another backcountry tour in this area of the Green Mountain National Forest, try the Pine Brook tour (see Chapter 12).

A little farther afield, the Texas Falls Recreation Area allows you access to the Bread Loaf Wilderness, which has miles of skiable roads. To get there, go north on VT 100 to Hancock and turn west on VT 125. Travel 2.5 miles, where there is a Forest Service sign for the recreation area at the junction with a Forest Service road on the north side of VT 125. Texas Falls was one of the many places I was sorry not to be able to include in this book—a fun place to ski. The U.S. Forest Service Rochester Ranger District Office (Route 100, Rochester, Vermont 05767; telephone: 802-767-4777) may be able to suggest other good backcountry skiing in this area.

PINE BROOK TRAIL

Rochester

Difficulty: Intermediate
Distance: 4.3 miles
Map: USFS Rochester Ranger District Pine Brook Trail Map
(normally available at trailhead)

This tour involves a long, difficult climb, which results in a great downhill run at the end of the trail. The uphill part requires only a willingness to work, the price you pay for great downhill runs in cross-country skiing (perhaps why this sport hasn't attracted the thousands that flock to downhill ski areas).

You are in very high country for part of this tour and much of the country has been logged. Consequently you get great views; some of the best of all the tours in this book. The Forest Service maintains the trails here, and they are well kept. The downhill section is on a very wide (two lane) road, making control very easy. You can turn from side to side, which helps cut your speed.

Access

From the west and VT 7, turn east on VT 73 at Brandon and travel 13 miles. From the east take VT 73 west off VT 100 just south of Rochester and go 3.9 miles. The turn for Forest Road 42 is obvious. It is on a sharp corner at a bridge and is well marked. The road is on the north side of VT 73. The parking area is 2 miles down Forest Road 42.

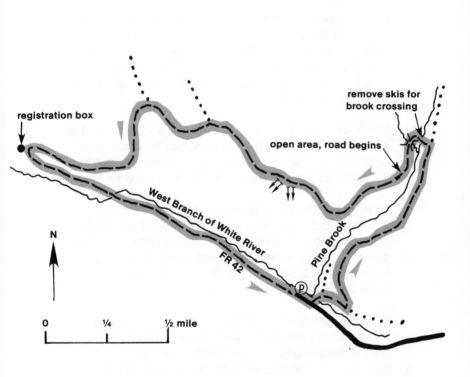

The Tour

After parking, leaving maximum space in this small parking area, ski across the bridge. There is a sign identifying the trail just before the bridge. Check out the clear water in the brook, the West Branch of the White River.

At the Y above, turn right. There is a house on the left. Climb slightly, past some old apple trees and into a grove of red pines. Continue to slab across the hill to the next intersection, a Y. Turn sharply left and ski through a gate. There is a sign marking the trail for use by skiers, hikers, and hunters.

Climb steeply out of the red pines and into birches. It is amazing how much the sun can soften the snow, even when the air is well below freezing. I skied this tour in the afternoon, and the snow on this slope was mushy.

There are some views behind you as you ascend the first crest, but they are only a small taste of what is to come. Ahead is a dense, dark stand of hemlocks. The canopy is so thick here that there is very little snow under the trees, and what is there is very hard; but these conditions don't last long.

The hill drops steeply off to your left. The climb is long enough to require you to take off a layer of clothes. Back in hardwoods, you get better views behind you. Stop for a minute and listen to the brook below. If the wind isn't blowing, it is the only sound you hear.

I came across some large and quite fresh moose tracks on this section. The moose came out of the brook, followed the trail a bit, and then climbed toward the crest of the hill to the right. The state of Vermont is trying to decide whether to have an open season on moose. The game wardens believe that there are thousands of these animals in the state; the biologists say there are

Pine Brook

hundreds. If you encounter one of these animals, treat it with great respect. They are quite unpredictable. A cow with a calf should be treated with particular caution.

Ski across several diversion ditches. The trail takes relaxed turns left and right. The other side of the valley comes closer and closer as you approach the top of the hill.

A sign at the next intersection indicates that you should continue skiing to the left. Cross Pine Brook ahead, which is large enough to require you to remove your skis. Ski up to another brook. You will see a small, rustic bridge on the right. Cross the brook and climb up to the crest of the hill before putting on your skis again. Turn left toward the open area.

I was sitting on the bank above the bridge taking pictures when I heard noises from above. Two mink were chasing each other over the snow. They were a beautiful, dark brown color that stood out against the snow.

From here on, most of the tour is flat or downhill. Ski to the open area and cross it to reach the beginning of a road, which you follow gradually to the right. A grove of red pine stands above you as the road climbs a slight grade. I saw many fox tracks in the area. Ski around the corner and into a lovely gravel pit.

Here are some great views to the south and west. Another large, open area around the corner gives you even more impressive views well worth the whole climb.

A trail leaves on the right, but follow the sign for the Pine Brook Trail. This area might be worth exploring, for there are many old roads going off this main one. Swing right into a grove of evergreens. There is another forest gate with no sign ahead. The road is so obvious that there aren't even any blazes alongside it. Another side trail goes uphill away from the road.

Continue downhill, a really enjoyable run. At the next intersection, take the time to record your passage at the registration box. It will help the Forest Service decide whether to add more trails for us to use.

Turn sharply left and ski along the brook on unplowed Forest Road 42. You cross the West Branch once more before you reach your car, a little over 1 mile down the road.

A rustic bridge crosses a small stream

Other Places to Ski

Austin Brook makes a good companion tour for Pine
Brook. It is located north on VT 100, 6.8 miles north of
Granville and 3.5 miles south of Warren. There is a parking lot on the side of VT 100, and the trail entrance is on
the west side of the road. The sign announces that you
are accessing the Bread Loaf Wilderness Area. The tour
runs "out and back," mostly uphill on the way in, with a
long downhill run on the way back out. The Chittenden
Brook Trail (see Chapter 11) is on VT 73, less than 4
miles west of where you turned off for this tour. The U.S.
Forest Service Rochester Ranger District Office (Route
100, Rochester, Vermont 05767; telephone: 802-767-
4777) may be able to suggest other good backcountry
skiing in this area.

13 BLUEBERRY HILL

Goshen

Difficulty: Intermediate
Distance: 5 miles
Map: Blueberry Hill Cross Country Ski Area Trail Map

This ski center has long had an exceptional reputation on several counts. The great trails and great food were well known and made this a destination resort. Although the center has had a somewhat lower profile recently, the quality of the experience hasn't changed. It is a great place to spend a day or a weekend, and it is close to Rikert and Mountain Top ski centers as well.

Access

From the west, take US 7 to East Middlebury. Turn onto VT 125 east toward Hancock. Nearly a mile past the town of Ripton, turn right on a Forest Service Road, FR 32. The turn is well marked with ski area signs. From the east, take VT 100 to Hancock and turn west on VT 125. After passing the Bread Loaf Campus of Middlebury College, take a left on the well-marked FR 32. Blueberry Hill is 5.2 miles south of VT 125 on FR 32.

Blueberry Hill can also be reached from the south via VT 73. Just 3.9 miles east of Brandon (or 14 miles west of the junction with VT 100), turn north off VT 73 onto the road to Goshen. Follow this road through the village of Goshen and turn left 1.4 miles after leaving VT 73. Follow this road for another 1.4 miles to an intersection. Turn right and drive 1.3 miles to Blueberry Hill.

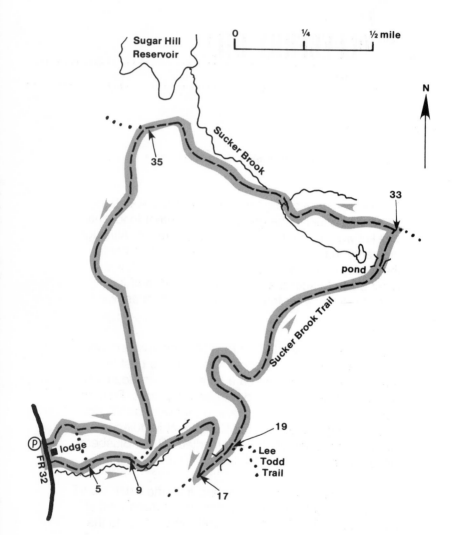

The Tour

From the ski shop, where you pay your trail fee, walk
across the road. You can see where the ski trails start
beside the lodge. Put on your skis and cross the dam
on the edge of the pond. You are now on Sucker Brook
Trail, and there is a brook below you on the right. At intersection 5, continue on Sucker Brook. The stream
below you is quite active and probably has some trout in
it. The trail flattens and swings away from the brook,
moving through small growth. A swamp appears on your
left. Swamps (and we see several on this tour) allow the
streams to flow all summer. The bogs, made up of
spongy vegetation, hold the water from the spring snow-
melt and the spring and summer seepage coming off
the mountains. Beavers also help keep the streams flowing. With their dams, they create ponds that hold water
and release it slowly.

At intersection 9, take a right turn, still on Sucker Brook.
Signs here also point the way to Goshen Dam. Ski
slightly downhill and into another swampy area. Views
open up off the ridge above you. Notice the dark evergreens on top. The small, bushy plants growing in the
swamp are alders.

Ski to the base of the hill, turn right, and climb. There is
a Green Mountain National Forest sign on the edge of
the trail just before intersection 17. At the intersection,
take a left and climb. You can see to the west and south
across several ridges of mountains, toward New York.
Continue over a bridge and up to intersection 19, where
the Lee Todd Trail leaves to the right. Ski straight,
through a dip and up the other side. Slab along a hill,
looking below you where there is another swamp and
open area. The views in the distance are engaging.

The trail switchbacks, which saves you some steep
climbs. (A straight trail that climbs for any distance gets

The trails start behind the Inn

washed out every time it rains.) As I skied this trail, I noticed how "dirty" the snow gets from contaminants in the air, as well as from the trees. Each of those little dark specks serves as a heat sink, absorbing heat from the sun and melting the snow.

You now ski left through a gap and over a height of land. Swing over the crest and down to the left on a quick downhill. The trail goes back toward the right and into hardwoods.

Slab across the hill. A clear-cut area is visible on a hill to the right through the trees. Stop for a minute and listen;

the day I was here, there was no sound, not even of wind in the trees. Ski hard to the left. A logging road enters on the right, although all you can see is a vague indentation in the snow. Colors reflect off the yellow birches along here, and buds are out on many of the trees in late February. Ski over a bridge near a pond that is visible through the trees on your left.

When you reach intersection 33, you are about halfway through your tour. Turn left here. The right trail goes to Bread Loaf. Continue on Sucker Brook, which is forty or fifty feet wide here. After the trail narrows a bit, it reaches a cleared area. Ski around the edge of the clearing, gradually to the right and then to the left. Clear-cuts are areas where all the trees have been cut for forestry products. They somehow always come as a surprise: You suddenly ski from deep woods into a huge, open area.

After a quick dip, the trail goes back to the right. Enjoy the many evergreens and the brook below you on the right. The trail is like a smooth boulevard. A large pond appears on the right—Sugar Hill Reservoir. You are about to turn back toward the lodge.

At intersection 35, turn left and climb, skiing through an area of broken trees; it looks like a bad storm has passed through here. Some nice views open up on your right. You are now on a bench between a steep hill on the left and a slope on the right. The trees squeak in the wind here. Turn sharply right and go downhill between white birches of ever-increasing size. At the next intersection, which has no number, turn right and climb slightly on an easy grade. Continue skiing in what appears to be overgrown fields. The trail swings left and goes downhill. At the next corner, where there is an old car, turn right. Keep skiing toward the left and downhill until you see the lodge ahead.

Other Places to Ski

Just down the road is Churchill House, where there is a lodge and cross-country ski area. The lodge is on VT 73, about 4 miles east of Brandon. The trail system connects with the trails at Blueberry Hill. Try the Ridge Trail; it is listed as a most difficult trail but is well worth trying if you have the skill. Two excellent backcountry tours, The Widow's Clearing Trail and Wilkinson Trails (see Chapters 14 and 15), are about 3 miles north of Blueberry Hill on Forest Road 32.

14 WIDOW'S CLEARING SKI TRAIL
Ripton

Difficulty: Intermediate

Distance: 6 miles

Map: USFS Middlebury Ranger District Winter Sports Trails Map (normally available ar trailhead)

A great backcountry tour requires nice scenery, good terrain, and, for me, a great downhill. This tour has all these elements.

The trip covers part of the Catamount Trail and can be used to connect the Blueberry Hill Ski Center with Rikert at Bread Loaf. If you do start at either of these centers, please remember to let the area know if you are going to leave your car, even if you are not planning to be out overnight. You will be expected to pay a trail fee. You can also start from either end of the tour at official Forest Service parking lots, although the tour description here starts from the lot on Forest Road 67.

Access

Take VT 125 from US 7 near East Middlebury or, in the east, from VT 100 at Hancock. Forest Road 67 is 3.5 miles east of Ripton and 8.2 miles west of Hancock on the south side of VT 125. The parking lot for the Widow's Clearing Trail is a little less than a mile down the forest road on the left. You might have to carry your skis until you get to skiable snow.

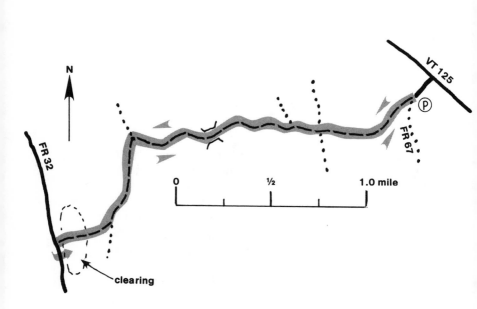

clearing

The Tour

From the parking area, start skiing to your right, following Forest Road 67. If the route has been used for logging, you will have to walk a short distance, but it isn't far to skiable snow. A sign on the left marks the start of the trail and indicates that you are 5.2 kilometers (3.2 miles) from Forest Road 32, the turnaround point for this tour. The trail is clearly marked throughout with the blue Catamount blazes.

The beginning of the trail is fairly steep, climbing through a dense grove of red pines. Ski across several water diversion ditches, which create quick ups and downs and can throw you off balance. They are put in to keep rainwater from washing the road away.

On the right side of the road is an open area probably logged some time ago. Several outgrown roads enter the one you are skiing on; our route keeps climbing gradually to the right.

As you ski out of the pines, views open up on your right. You can just see the roofs of the buildings at the Bread Loaf Campus of Middlebury College. Climb slightly left to a major road crossing. Blue blazes should be discernible straight ahead; follow the blazes. An old stone wall appears on your right, the first one on this tour.

A large open area appears above you. Ski along the bottom edge of it and back into the woods. At the right edge of the clearing, there is a Y in the trail. It is obvious that you take the left branch, for there are many blazes on the trees. Climb slightly, then ski on flat terrain for a bit. You are in open hardwoods, and there is evidence of a lot of animal activity in this area. Ski up and down with no major changes in direction. If the snow has been packed by previous skiers, you will be able to double-pole this section. Turn left and climb slightly onto another shelf. Cross a small brook on a snow-covered bridge. A slight downhill ends at a sharp ditch. Such obstacles provide good reasons to keep your speed under control in the backcountry.

The trail climbs left, right, then left again. Continue along a flat section. Check out the large stumps that might be visible; some fair-sized trees were cut in this area. Beware of the extraneous blue blazes on trees off the trail on your right. Perhaps they were to mark the edge of a logging area or a survey line.

When you start down to the right, note the large boulder on the left side of the trail with trees growing on it: Another warning to control your speed. Just ahead is a bridge that goes over a brook. Take it slowly, taking care not to slide off and into the brook.

The trail continues around to the right. You can still see some blazes off in the woods. Climb to the left and then reach slightly flatter terrain. You have now attained the great divide and are 1 mile from the turnaround point. Ski up and around the edge of a hill that rises above you on the right. The tour is now on a fairly substantial road. Continue around the hill and down slightly. At the Y intersection with signs, make a hard left and follow the ski trail markers. The Y is not on the Forest Service map.

After a quick dip, the trail flattens out and makes for easy skiing. There were lots of animal tracks in here. In fact, I followed fox tracks through most of this trip.

Slab along the side of the hill on your left and over a small brook. Turn sharply right at the next set of signs. Ski down and around a small knob on your left that is covered with evergreens. When the trail takes a sharp dip downhill, you will see Widow's Clearing ahead. Cross the clearing through its center. The blazes are on

A Forest Service sign marks the start of the trail

posts. When you reach the trees on the other side, you will see the trail swinging to the right. Ski along the left edge of the clearing and climb easily. The parking lot on Forest Service Road 32 is visible as you turn back to the left.

Return via the same trail to your car on Forest Road 67.

Other Places to Ski

You are minutes from Blueberry Hill and Rikert ski centers (see Chapters 13 and 17). The Wilkinson Trails (see Chapter 15) adjoin this tour, and there are several other backcountry opportunities in the Middlebury-Hancock area. Check with the U.S. Forest Service Middlebury Ranger District Office (RD #4, Box 1260, Middlebury, Vermont 05753; telephone: 802-388-4362) for winter trail maps and the latest information on conditions.

15 WILKINSON SKI TRAILS

Ripton

Difficulty: Novice/Intermediate
Distance: 5 miles
Map: USFS Middlebury Ranger District Williamson Ski Trails Map (normally available at trailhead)

This area of the Green Mountain National Forest contains many trails, perhaps a reaction to demand from the Middlebury area. The Wilkinson Trails are part of a new system (1989). A pocket map is available for free, although the Forest Service does ask for donations. If enough people donate, perhaps the Forest Service will clear and mark additional trails.

The trail described here is skiable by anyone with a good snowplow technique and the ability to turn his or her skis. The trail rolls easily for most of its length and does not require any long climbs. Cutoff trails will allow you to cut your tour short if you find the skiing difficult.

Access

To reach the trailhead, take VT 125 from US 7 south of Middlebury, or pick up VT 125 at Hancock from VT 100. Travel 5 miles east on VT 125, or 11 miles west from Hancock, to Forest Service Road 32, which goes south nearly a mile east of Ripton. Follow the Forest Service road 2.5 miles to the Widow's Clearing parking lot on the left.

The Tour

Across the road from the parking lot, the trail for Black-

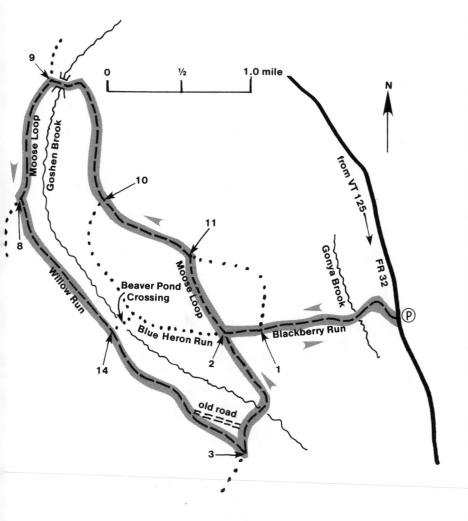

berry Run goes sharply downhill in an open, cutover area. If the snow cover is thin, don't worry, for there is usually better cover on the other side of this valley. Swing left, and when you reach the bottom, watch for the brook; it can surprise you, for the steep bank is hard to see. The trail climbs up the other side of the valley toward the right. It is clear where the trail gets its name: There are blackberry bushes everywhere.

Ahead, the trail swings hard to the right. When you reach intersection 1, ski toward the left. Climb up a bit and head right. Small trees line the trail. At intersection 2, take a right onto Moose Loop and climb slightly.

Climb up with moderate steepness to intersection 11, and continue straight on Moose Loop. You have now crested the hill and are going downhill. The trees are very small here, and signs of wildlife are prevalent along the trail. Swing left and down more sharply. An old road enters on the left, and the trail flattens a bit.

At the next intersection, number 10, ski straight through on Moose Loop. The trail snakes downhill and around to the left. A caution sign warns of a sharp corner to the left. At the bottom is a narrow bridge over a major brook; take it very slowly. Check out the old bridge beams below the new structure: They are huge. At the next intersection, number 9, take a sharp left, still on Moose Loop. The trail to the right goes out of the area to another access point.

Climb steeply, then a little more easily on a good road. You are now surrounded by large forest growth, mostly hardwoods. At intersection 8, about 2½ miles from the start of the tour, Moose Loop heads toward the right. Take Willow Run instead, continuing along the side of a hill and through a clearing. You can see a beaver pond on your left. The next intersection is marked 14, Beaver

The start of an excellent Forest Service Trail system

Pond Crossing. You are more than halfway through your tour. You can shorten the tour by taking Beaver Pond Crossing to Blue Heron Run, where you turn right to reach Blackberry Run again. It is a ten-minute ski across the beaver pond, less than a third of a mile. Otherwise, keep skiing straight on Willow.

There may be some wet areas on the trail here. Ice will form immediately on the bottoms of your skis if you accidently slide over water. You will have to stop and scrape them clean again. If you don't have a scraper, use the side of your pole basket.

View across the valley from the start of the Wilkinson Trail system

Continue skiing along the beaver pond. At the next Y with an old road, ski uphill—a pretty good climb. At intersection 3, Moose Loop comes back in on your right. Turn left, following the signs for the parking lot.

The trail swings left and then right. It is wide and smooth but fairly steep. Yellow birches line the route. After a short climb, you will reach the intersection (number 2) where you started the loop. Turn right on Blackberry and ski back toward the parking lot. At intersection 1, head right. (Don't forget the ditch at the bottom of the open area!)

Other Places to Ski

The Widow's Clearing Trail (see Chapter 14) is just across Forest Service Road 32 from the starting point of this tour. Other skiing is available at the Rickert Ski Touring Center at Middlebury College's Bread Loaf Campus (see Chapter 17) and at Blueberry Hill (see Chapter 13), further south on Forest Service Road 32. There are several other backcountry trails in this area. The best guide to them is the Winter Sports Trail Map put out by the U.S. Forest Service Middlebury Ranger District Office (RD #4, Box 1260, Middlebury, Vermont 05753; telephone: 802-388-4362).

16 MT. TOM
Woodstock

Difficulty: Intermediate
Distance: 6 miles
Map: Woodstock Ski Touring Center Trail Map

Woodstock, Vermont, was a destination for the rich during the last part of the nineteenth century. It is still visited by many tourists looking for that special Vermont experience. The town is filled with interesting shops providing much after-ski entertainment. Skiing has been a much-practiced sport here since the 1930s when the first rope tow in the United States was built. When cross-country skiing became popular, the townsfolk saw its potential. The golf course serves as a perfect area for skiing, with the country club building as the base of operations.

Another area in the town is also used for skiing and is operated as part of the touring center. Mt. Tom has been a managed forest since the late 1800s. In fact, it was the first tree farm in Vermont. The mountain was owned by railroad magnate and environmentalist Frederick Billings. He built miles of carriage roads there that today make for wonderful skiing.

Access

The trails are operated out of the touring center on VT 106, just south of town. You must check in at the center, pay your fee, and get a trail map. The route to the ski

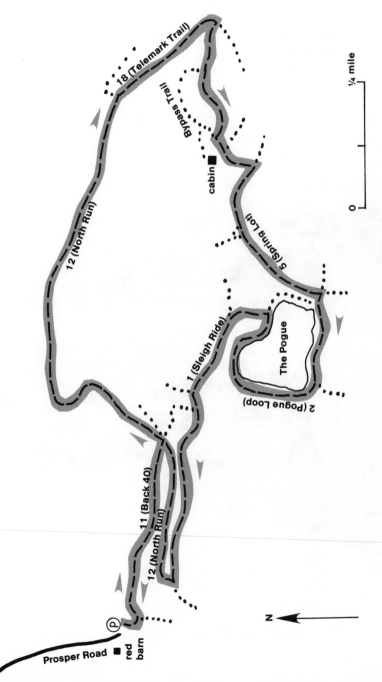

18 (Telemark Trail)

Bypass Trail

cabin

12 (North Run)

5 (Spring Lot)

1 (Sleigh Ride)

The Pogue

2 (Pogue Loop)

11 (Back 40)

12 (North Run)

Prosper Road

red barn

P

N

¼ mile

0

touring area on Mt. Tom is detailed on the map available at the center. You will be skiing from the Prosper-West Woodstock Road parking lot.

View to the east from Mt. Tom

The Tour

Ski to the far end of the parking lot, away from the entrance. The trail climbs steeply, then flattens out in a stand of pines. Ski to the first intersection and go left on 11, Back 40. The trail is flat, but then turns sharply left and climbs a hill. You can see two large trees, one dead and one alive, that are hollow. They provide hiding places for animals and birds. A beautiful pine forest spreads out on both sides of the trail. The trees are set far apart, differing from what you would see in an unmanaged forest. As a result, the trees do not block out all the sun, and the understory flourishes.

The trail swings right and climbs more steeply. It continues by moving toward the left and climbing more gradually. A large maple split by lightning stands on the left side of the trail.

You might see turkey tracks along the trail. Turkeys were almost wiped out in New England as a game bird, but they have been successfully reintroduced. Seeing them is a thrill, but it doesn't happen very often since they are very shy birds. They fly at the first sign of people, and they can run with amazing speed. Flocks can include a dozen or more birds.

The trail signs are small but easy to read. At the next intersection, take a left onto 12, North Run. Check the map. The contour lines, the light brown ones, show that you are skiing around the edge of the hill. You will ski down and then up again in mixed evergreens and birches. You can see the beginnings of a brook on your left and a steep slope on the right.

The ridge top is visible ahead as you swing back to the left. There are expansive views to the north toward Barnard. As the trail swings back to the right, there are also views to the east of rolling hills.

Climb slightly, then start downhill, slabbing across the side of the hill. There are few animal signs here possibly because animals avoid the mountain's cold northerly exposure. It receives little sunlight.

Ski downhill through hardwoods. You will be able to hear VT 12 and perhaps the downhill ski area on the other side of the valley. Climb somewhat, the hill above you steepening. There is a sugaring operation here; you can see the plastic pipe in the trees. Originally the sap was collected in metal buckets and carried down to the sugarhouse for boiling. It is very steep here, however, and I wonder if this area was tapped before gravity feed systems became available. If so, it must have been a lot of work.

Start down a steeper grade through evergreens. Several other sap pipes go over the trail. The trail is so protected by the hill here that snow conditions are quite different from the rest of the trail system. The evergreens along this section are hemlock, a shade-loving tree. Across the valley are pines: a sun-loving species.

The next intersection is the Telemark Trail, 18. It goes down to the VT 12 access point. Turn right up the hill. Ski up to and over a snow-covered road with a barbed wire fence on one side. You are still in the open. This is a great telemark ski hill. You could ski all the way to the road, cutting lovely turns in the classic telemark style.

At a Y intersection, take the right fork, still on Telemark Trail. There are some big white birches on the right as you climb. Bypass Trail leaves our trail to the right. Climbing a bit more, you will see the cabin ahead, 2.5 miles from the start of the tour. At the cabin, ski left between the cabin and the outhouse. They actually groom the path to the outhouse. The cabin is impressive, twenty by thirty feet with a wood stove and sundeck. It is

Well-groomed trails through carefully managed woods are characteristic of the Woodstock area

a great place for lunch. The view from the deck is of a beautiful, round-topped hill.

From the front of the cabin, ski to the bottom of the field and into evergreens. Turn sharply right. You are on number 5, Spring Lot. Big maples line the lane ahead; the summer pasture is on the left. Swing left at the next intersection and ignore the next trail to the right. Beech trees stand on the right; the barbed wire fence on the left looks new. You ski past a swampy section on the left and then across a flat section through small trees. You are headed toward the Pogue, a pond once believed to have a quicksand bottom. At one time, the Pogue provided the water supply for the Billings Farm, now a working museum, at the foot of Mt. Tom. You can see the Pogue through the trees, but the trail swings away from it.

At the next intersection, a horse watering trough cut out of stone is on the left. Take a right on the Pogue Loop. You are now skiing around the edge of the pond. There is an impressive set of ledges above you. Ski along the base of a steep slope and head back into evergreens. When you reach Sleigh Ride, you are a short half hour of easy downhill skiing, about 1.5 miles, from the parking lot. Turn left. At the next Y, turn left. You are now skiing back and above the Pogue. At the next intersection, take another left. The trail is now slightly sloping, and there are views to the north of rolling hills. Stop in an open area and enjoy the view. When you get to 12, turn sharply right onto North Run. The trail ahead rolls up and down. When you get to the next crosstrail, turn left and ski back to the parking lot.

Other Places to Ski

Skiing at the main complex in Woodstock is also excellent. According to the staff, the skiing on the golf course is good on a very small amount of snow. The mountain trails that are connected to the golf course are challenging, so you can get in both novice and expert skiing. I've practiced skating there on tracks groomed to perfection during very difficult skiing conditions. The touring center can also provide a map of the ungroomed Skyline Trail, just north of Woodstock in Pomfret. Although some sections have been affected by construction, parts of it still offer fine backcountry skiing and magnificent views.

17 RIKERT SKI TOURING CENTER

Ripton

Difficulty: Novice/Intermediate
Distance: 3 miles
Map: Rikert Ski Touring Center Map

This touring center on the western slope of the Green Mountains owes its existence to Middlebury College and its ski team. Although the area is maintained for public use, here is where some of the best ski racers in the country train. It has also been the sight of the NCAA National Cross-Country Skiing Championships.

The town of Middlebury was established in the 1820s and, for a time, was the largest population center on the western slope, its citizens outnumbering those of Rutland, Bennington, and even Burlington. The Bread Loaf Campus of Middlebury College, where this center is located, is home to the well-known Bread Loaf Writers Conference during the summer. The buildings were part of a hotel complex owned by Joseph Battell, who also established the Vermont Morgan Horse Farm north of Middlebury. The horse farm is operated by the University of Vermont.

Battell bequeathed thirty-thousand acres to Middlebury College, including the land that makes up the Bread Loaf complex. He was, at one point in his life, the largest landowner in Vermont.

Access
To get to the center, take VT 125 off US 7, traveling

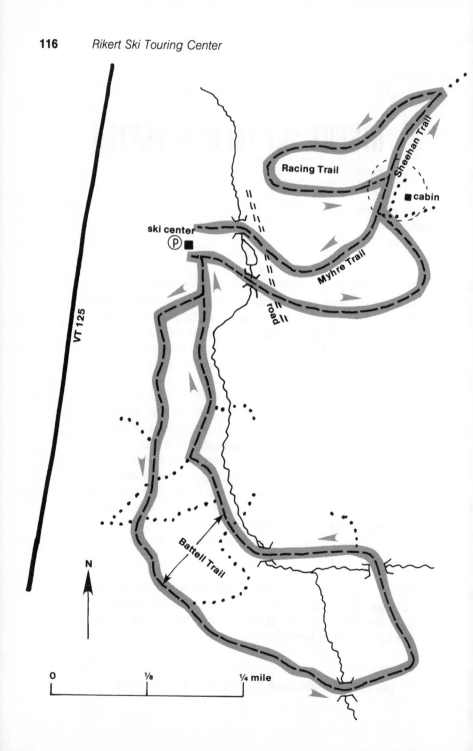

Racing Trail

Sheehan Trail

■ cabin

ski center
Ⓟ ■

Myhre Trail

road

VT 125

Battell Trail

N

0   ⅛   ¼ mile

through East Middlebury and Ripton. The center is 3 miles past Ripton. From the east, take VT 100 to Hancock and go west on VT 125. Rikert is 1.5 miles beyond the Middlebury College Snow Bowl.

The center of operations is in the basement of a large, barnlike building on the right side of the parking lot.

The Tour

After you have checked in, paid your trail fee, and found out what trails are open, head to the right from the center complex and into the large field. The tour is broken into two halves. This first section is easy skiing, with gradual ups and downs and wide trails, and is suitable for anyone with a strong snowplow. Signs along the way suggest what ski techniques are appropriate for the terrain.

Ski around the field to the left and toward a large, white house. When you reach a sign marked the Battell Trail, turn left and ski into the woods. After a short climb, the trail opens up into a small meadow. Another trail goes off on the right. Stay straight. You are still on the B Trail.

The center has tacked trail maps to the trees at major intersections. Any confusion can be easily clarified by a quick check of this map. Your current position is always marked with an arrow. More areas could certainly benefit by using this method of trail identification.

The center also kindly provides signs identifying some of the natural history of the area you are skiing through. This spot is old pastureland. Vermont, once 75 percent pasture and cleared land, is now 75 percent forest. These small, open areas provide grazing for deer and smaller animals, while the brush surrounding them is good cover and protection from the weather and predators.

Bear claw marks on a beech tree

The B Trail is also marked as the route of the Catamount Trail. Other sections of this state-long trail appear in several of the other tours in this book. Bower Trail comes in on the left.

Dead branches on the ground provide cover for small animals, and, as they decay, they feed the plants and trees still living. Insects, mushrooms and other fungi, and bacteria help break down the wood. Water and frost action also helps.

A major snowmobile route touches the trail as you turn back toward the lodge. Ski over a bridge and keep heading toward the lodge. Another, much smaller snowmobile trail touches the trail as you ski over another brook.

Ski back into a spruce forest. The Catamount Trail leaves on the Freeman Trail, to the right, on its way to Lincoln Gap and the Canadian border. Stay on the B Trail. Signs now indicate that you are headed back toward Bread Loaf.

The brook on your left flows into Otter Creek and Lake Champlain, out the Richleau River in Canada, into the St. Lawrence, and thus to the North Atlantic.

Several trails connect with this one, but ignore them and ski up and over a short incline to a Y intersection. Go toward the right, still following signs to Bread Loaf. Caution signs are placed on the downhill ahead. After a short flat, you will ski back up into the field, with the ski center ahead. The loop you finished is technically quite easy.

The next half of the tour is more difficult, with steep uphills and downhills. From the front of the lodge, ski down a slope to the right of the shed and cross the East

Bread Loaf Mountain

Middlebury River. Ski over the road and go uphill on the
Racing Trail through spruces. Watch for small birds
feeding in the bushes along the trail. The trail climbs up
to the left and into a grove of hardwoods. There is a
complicated intersection ahead with a cabin above it.
Keep to the top of the open area and slab across the hill
on J, the Sheehan Trail. After about 100 yards, the
Sheehan Trail crosses the Intercollegiate Racing Trail;
stay on the Sheehan Trail. After a little more than ⅛ mile,
there is another junction with the Intercollegiate Racing
Trail. Here, you turn sharply left and downhill onto the

Racing Trail, which soon swings to the right. The trail is wide enough to snowplow comfortably, but it is a significant downhill. The trail reaches a dip and climbs back up to the Sheehan Trail. Turn sharply right onto the Sheehan Trail and follow it for about 100 yards until you come back to the complicated intersection. Turn right here onto M, the Mhyre Trail (not signed when I skied it), and ski down the hill on a wide trail. Swing right over the road and river. The center is visible ahead.

Other Places to Ski

With more than thirty miles of trails, Rikert offers a variety of other routes suitable for all ability levels. In addition, you are only minutes from two outstanding backcountry tours, Widow's Clearing and Wilkinson trails (see Chapters 14 and 15). There are several other backcountry opportunities in the Middlebury-Ripton area. Check with the U.S. Forest Service Ranger District Office (RD #4, Box 1260, Middlebury, VT 05753; telephone: 802-388-4362) for winter trail maps and the latest information on conditions.

18

OLE'S CROSS-COUNTRY CENTER
West Warren

Difficulty:	Intermediate
Distance:	8 miles
Map:	Ole's Cross-Country Center Map

The Mad River Valley area near Waitsfield, Vermont, is justifiably famous for downhill skiing, with Mad River Glen, Sugarbush, and Sugarbush North all located there. The towns of Waitsfield and Warren are geared to serving tourists in all seasons and skiers in particular. Wonderful lodges, mountainside condos, and small bed and breakfast inns are set beside the roaring Mad River and its tributaries. As a destination resort for a winter trip, you couldn't pick a better location. Although the main focus of the area is on downhill skiing, cross-country skiing is exceptional. You can ski a different area or trail each day for a week and try a different restaurant every night.

Access

The tour we will do here is at Ole's Cross Country Ski Center located at the Sugarbush Airport. To get to the center, go to Warren Village just off VT 100 and take the eastbound route out of the village on Brook Road. After following Brook Road up the hill for 2 miles, you will come to the junction with the road to Blueberry Lake, which goes to the right. Bear left on the main road and follow it another .5 mile to East Warren. Turn left in East Warren, across from the Roxbury Notch Road. The air-

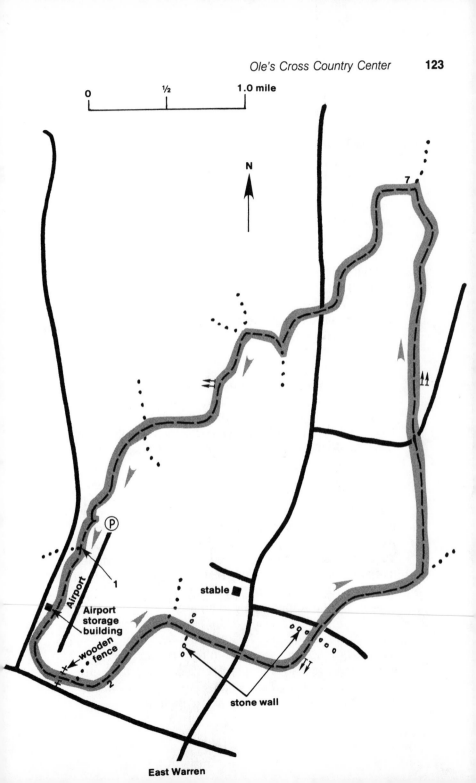

0   ½   1.0 mile

N

7

(P)

1

Airport

Airport
storage
building

wooden
fence

2

stable ■

stone wall

East Warren

port signs are easy to see, and Ole has also placed signs for the ski center, which is on the right .5 mile from the East Warren intersection.

Fees are paid in the ski center, located in the airport tower (which is not used for flying in the winter). The center runs a small snack bar, and rental equipment and other ski necessities are available.

The Tour

From the front of the center, ski right toward the silver building. At marker number 1, go left, following trail number 2. Ski around an airport storage building. The Waitsfield area is considered one of the best soaring centers in the East. Glider rides are available here during the summer months.

Looking left you can see Roxbury Gap, a dirt road that runs over the Northfield Mountain range and into the Dog River Valley. An old stage road over Braintree Gap just to the south of Roxbury Gap provides an interesting backcountry ski.

Ski into a dip and around to the left through a wooden fence. Ski sharply right on trail number 2, passing out of the field and over a small road. Go past a home on your right and into the woods on an old road. The trail complex Ole has put together uses miles of private property. You will be skiing past some lovely homes, most of them modern in style, but carefully placed and designed to fit into the area without intruding on the open mountain feeling. They add pleasingly to the view.

Ski back into a field and head right toward a large indoor riding ring and stable. Turn right through a stone wall. Follow the tracks around the field, first to the right and then to the left. In the fields, Ole sets tracks where the best snow settles, usually along the trees.

The airport control tower, used as a lodge in winter

Climb slightly to a tar road. Cross the road and ski up the edge of a field. A look behind you will reveal a great view over the valley. The Sugarbush Ski Area is furthest to the left, and the one on the right is Sugarbush North.

Turn left through the stone wall to reach a road. Cross it and continue uphill to the left. Views behind you now include Appalachian Gap, a sharp dip just north of Sugarbush North, and Lincoln Gap, just south of Sugarbush.

Ski through a gap in the stone wall near some old apple trees, the site of an old farm. Ahead the trail enters a dark spruce woods. A pair of big maples sit behind an old farm wagon. Turn sharply left along a flat section leading to a road, then ski downhill on the edge of the road. When the road meets another road, ski straight across and into a field. There is a tree-covered knoll ahead; keep it on your left. Stop by a gap in a stone wall and take time to enjoy the view. You can see the Mount Mansfield and Spruce Peak ski areas at Stowe, north of Waterbury and the Winooski River Valley.

After your break, go straight ahead along the edge of the field and through a row of pines. You can now see Camels Hump mountain in the northwest. The angle of your view makes it difficult to see the distinctive shape that gives the mountain its name. Although Camels Hump has always had treeless ledges on its top, the treeless area has grown in recent years due to acid rain. Because of its elevation, Camels Hump was one of the earliest places where acid rain damage was measurable.

Ski back into the woods, heading downhill. The trail swings and dips through a field and goes back left into the woods. Watch for trail number 7 leaving to the right, but do not take it.

A small outbuilding and a house stand to the right. Watch for the red and blue trail markers. The trail goes down a steep, narrow road with just enough room for a strong snowplow. It ends at the tar road.

The trail goes directly across the road, back into a field, and left behind an old barn. Ski to a trail junction. Turn right, going over a small brook and up a short, steep hill. Take a left where the sign says back to Ole's in 2 k's (1¼ miles).

Ski along the edge of the fence, and continue through a wire gate and into the next field. There are impressive views of Sugarbush ahead. Ski left along the field, then into the woods past a deformed old birch tree on your right. The woods here are filled with large spruce trees, which tend to make for uneven conditions; the falling snow can't get through the thick, evergreen branches. There are also some big maples in this woods.

A trail crosses your path, but go straight ahead, uphill and into the field. The ski center is just ahead.

Skiers enjoy the wide, rolling trails

Other Places to Ski

Tucker Hill Lodge in Waitsfield offers skiing, and a tour there can be combined with a ski to the Sugarbush Ski Center in Warren via the Catamount Trail. Blueberry Lake, which is just down the road from Ole's, also offers skiing. As mentioned above, the old stage road across Braintree Gap makes an interesting backcountry expedition. It is reached by a side road going east from Granville on VT 100 (see the DeLorme or Northern Cartographic atlas for details).

NORTHERN

19 CAMELS HUMP NORDIC SKI CENTER

Huntington

Difficulty: Intermediate
Distance: 7 miles
Map: Camels Hump Nordic Ski Center Map

This touring center is set high above the Huntington River Valley, the mountain known as Camels Hump rising behind it. At 4083 feet high, Camels Hump is the tallest peak in Vermont without a ski area. The center typically has a good snow cover, and the lodge is small and comfortable. The owners also run a bed and breakfast.

Access

From I-89, take exit 11 and head toward Richmond. In the center of Richmond, turn right, cross the river, then turn right again and travel 6.5 miles to Huntington; there are a few side roads, but stay on the obvious main road. You can also approach Huntington from the south via VT 17. The road to Huntington is just west of the mountains and is well marked. In the center of Huntington, turn east (there are ski center signs). There are several turns as you climb toward the center, but the turns are well marked. Continue to follow the ski center signs. The parking lot is located well below the lodge, which is up a steep road. Take all your ski gear with you as you head up. There is also a lower parking lot, but try the top one first.

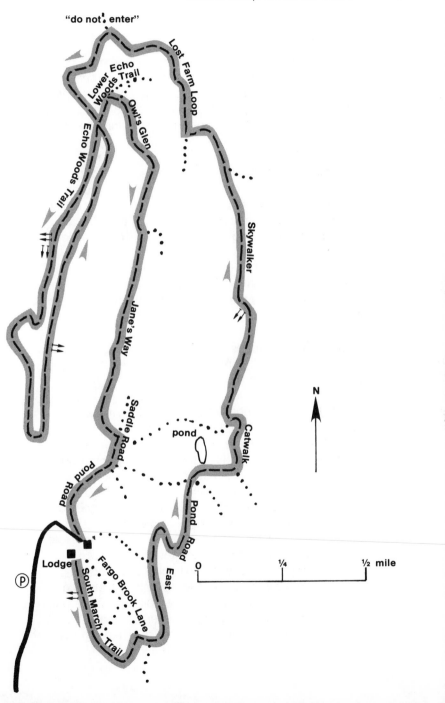

"do not enter"

Lost Farm Loop

Lower Echo Woods Trail

Owl's Glen

Echo Woods Trail

Skywalker

Jane's Way

Saddle Road

pond

Catwalk

N

Pond Road

Pond Road East

Fargo Brook Lane

Lodge

P

South March Trail

0   ¼   ½ mile

The Tour

Take the South March Trail after leaving the main building. Ski slightly downhill and through a fence, heading
toward a stone wall slightly to your left. There are some
nice views toward Lake Champlain and the Adiron-
dacks. The sloping section of field just before the woods
is a good place to practice your downhill technique.

The trail climbs to the left to an intersection. Continue
straight on South March. The lodge is still visible on the
left. At the next intersection, turn right, down into a little
dip and over a bridge. You are now on Fargo Brook
Lane. Swing left, going slightly uphill. A trail to the lower
parking lot goes to the right. Ski to a Y intersection,
where you take Pond Road East to the right. Swing to
the left on a fairly flat section. You are climbing, making
switchbacks across the mountain and moving between
two brooks.

Sparkling white birches stand out against a blue sky as
you climb the hill. A pond, a flat area above the trail, is
visible ahead. Ski to a T intersection and turn right,
uphill, on Catwalk. A left will take you downhill back to
the center. After a short distance a trail leaves to the
right; bear left. The trail then swings back to the left. You
can see where there are water bars in the trail: these are
mounds of dirt used to force the water off the trail so
that it doesn't erode in the spring and summer.

Ski along a flat section. Leave Catwalk, which goes off
to your left, and go straight ahead on Skywalker. Skywalker goes downhill, then flattens out. There are excellent views down the valley, back toward the touring
center. A steep ravine lies below, and rocky ledges
hang above. More birches grow on both sides of the
trail. I saw bobcat tracks along the trail here. They look
like house cat prints, only larger. After you reach the top
of the grade, you can see down into a wild-looking val-

View of Camels Hump and the hills surrounding the touring center

ley toward the north. A little-used trail joins your trail from your right. Swing toward the right, then ski around a sharp, left-hand corner. At the next intersection, turn right onto Lost Farm Loop. You are now 2.5 miles from the lodge. Several logging roads enter the trail, but the main trail is easy to follow.

There are many partridge tracks here where brush piles provide good shelter for the birds. The trail goes to the right. A trail marked "do not enter" goes straight, so head left. Ski through a hollow and then, using S turns, climb very gradually.

Ski around to the left, where you can see the peaks surrounding Camels Hump. At the intersection ahead, Lower Echo Woods Trail goes left, downhill, and Echo Woods Trail, which makes a 2-mile loop, goes both straight ahead and to the right. Turn right to take the loop. The trail travels along the top of a knoll, first to the right, then back to the left. In several cutover sections, you can see first to the south toward Bristol, then west toward Lake Champlain. After skiing around the knoll, the views open up toward the east. You can also look down on the ski center complex. The dark green clump of fir trees to the east is where the pond lies and where Catwalk Trail starts. It is amazing how far you have climbed without doing much apparent work.

There is a spectacular view of Camels Hump from here. Its frosty, ice-covered top dominates the skyline to the east. Keep skiing around to the left and back to the intersection where the Echo Woods loop began. Take a right, downhill on the Lower Echo Trail. Ski down to the next intersection and take a sharp right on Owl's Glen. The trail goes fairly steeply downhill. You appear to be skiing down a brook. In places it feels like you are heading down a bobsled run with tight, sweeping corners. Owl's Glen ends at Jane's Way, where you turn right over a bridge. When you get to the next intersection, turn right on Saddle Road and then right on Pond Road. You can stay on this trail back to the touring center.

Other Places to Ski

The nearest good cross-country skiing is at Sherman Hollow (see Chapter 20). Bolton Valley Ski Area, off US 2 about 5 miles southeast of Richmond, has great skiing. To the east, the Waitsfield Valley offers good skiing at Tucker Hill Lodge, Blueberry Lake, and Ole's Cross Country Center (see Chapter 18).

SHERMAN HOLLOW
Huntington

Difficulty: Novice/Intermediate
Distance: 6.5 miles
Map: Sherman Hollow Touring Center Map

This center has one of the most developed and well-groomed trail systems in Vermont. Much effort and money has gone into making their trails very skiable, even with marginal weather conditions. I have been amazed at how much snow the hills here get. The valley might have very little snow, but by the time you climb the access road, good skiing snow prevails: and in less than two miles.

Access

Take I-89 to the Richmond/Bolton US 2 exit (exit 11). Turn south on US 2 toward Richmond. At the light in the center of Richmond, take a right. This is the road to Huntington, although you will turn off before reaching Huntington village. There are a few roads branching off, but the main road is obvious. The turn for Sherman Hollow Road is marked on your right, about 4.7 miles from Richmond, and about 1.8 miles short of Huntington. The touring center, which is on the same road as the Green Mountain Audubon Nature Center, is about 2 miles down the road.

The Tour

From the porch of the lodge where you purchase your

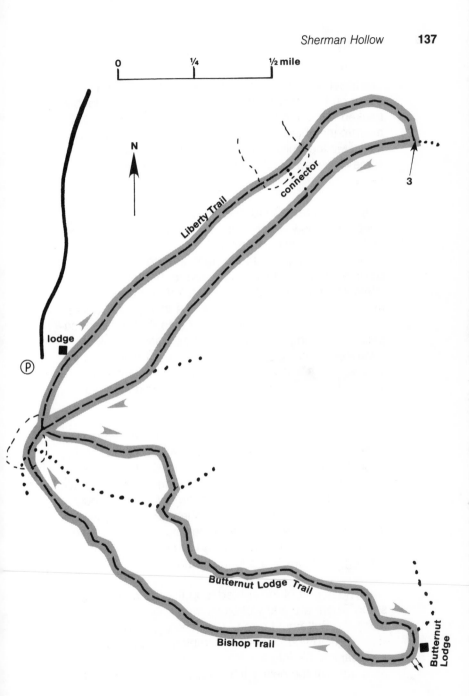

0   ¼   ½ mile

N

Liberty Trail

connector

3

lodge

P

Butternut Lodge Trail

Bishop Trail

Butternut Lodge

trail ticket, walk left and up to the ski trail. You will be skiing on the Liberty Trail. The trail is rolling and double tracked. Although the snow may be a little thin under the evergreens ahead, the underlying grassy ground cover facilitates the skiing. After a short downhill, you get some nice views of the hills on your left through the trees.

At an open area ahead, the views are downhill toward Sherman Hollow, where you can see the road and several houses. Continue across the top of the field and back into birches. Ski to the right, then to the left. A road goes left, but you continue up and to the right. At a T intersection (number 3), turn right. You are about 1½ miles from the lodge. Just below the trail is a dead tree with an interesting mottled appearance. In five large maples growing together along the trail, I saw a flock of grosbeaks working the upper branches. These birds are very colorful: yellow with contrasting black feathers. They are voracious eaters as anyone with a home feeder can attest to.

You are slabbing across the hill about a hundred feet above your outbound leg. A field is visible below through the trees. Continue to climb easily toward the lodge. A trail comes in on your left. After skiing up a little more steeply, you will see the lodge below you through the woods. Ski out into the field ahead and end your tour if you are a novice. The remaining 3.5 miles of the tour include more difficult skiing but reward you with some great views and a long downhill.

The field is part of the lighted loop that is used for night skiing. There are many choices from here. Turn left to reach the Butternut Lodge Trail. (There are some nice views behind you.) Continue climbing through birches and maples. Ski into a T intersection marked 6. Take a hard right. At the next Y intersection, which comes up

Sherman Hollow's trail system starts high above the valley floor

very quickly, take a left. The route is well marked as the
Butternut Lodge Trail. After skiing over a small knob
covered with large birches, you will meet the Champlain
Overlook Trail going to the left. You continue to the right.
The Butternut Lodge is off the trail on the left. Take time
to enjoy the views from the porch. You can get a perfect
view of Camels Hump across the valley. If you look
carefully, you can see the ski slope on the back side of
Mt. Ellen (Sugarbush North) over in the Waitsfield area.

Ski toward the right when you get back to the trail,
which is now called Bishop. You get some nice views off
the hill you are skiing on as you swing around to the
right. There are several large ledge systems above the
trail with large ice falls. Practice your snowplow to con-

trol your speed; you are going to need it. Continue skiing around the hill, spiraling down toward the lodge. A trail enters on the left, but if it hasn't been skied or cleared, you might not notice it. The trail finally flattens out at the field. The parking lot is ahead, and you can see the lodge.

Other Places to Ski

The Camels Hump Nordic Ski Center (See Chapter 19) is only a few miles away. The Bolton Valley Ski Area, reached by an access road that leaves US 2 about five miles southeast of Richmond, offers miles of highly scenic cross-country skiing—much of it through high wilderness terrain.

21
MT. MANSFIELD
Stowe

Difficulty: Novice/Intermediate
Distance: 7 miles
Map: Mt. Mansfield Cross-Country Ski Center Map

Stowe is one of the best known downhill ski areas in the East. Set in a snowy pocket of high mountains, it gets more than its share of the white stuff every winter. The Stowe region is also blessed with perfect terrain for cross-country skiing. The Mt. Mansfield Cross Country Ski Center is owned and operated by the same company that runs the downhill area.

Stowe is also the home of the oldest downhill–cross-country ski race in North America. The race began, in 1945, as a personal challenge from Sepp Ruschp, a transplanted Austrian ski champion, to Erling Strom, a renowned mountaineer. The challenge was to race from the top of the Toll Road on Mt. Mansfield to the village of Stowe, a distance of ten miles with a vertical drop of almost three thousand feet. The race combined downhill skiing on the mountain with cross-country skiing over the rolling terrain in the valley. Ruschp won the first race. The challenge was renewed as a public event each year until 1954. The racing event was revived in 1972 and now attracts as many as one thousand skiers. The terrain is tough, and conditions can be anything from powder to hard spring conditions. Held at the end of February, this race is a real test for any skier. Our tour starts at one of the access points to the race.

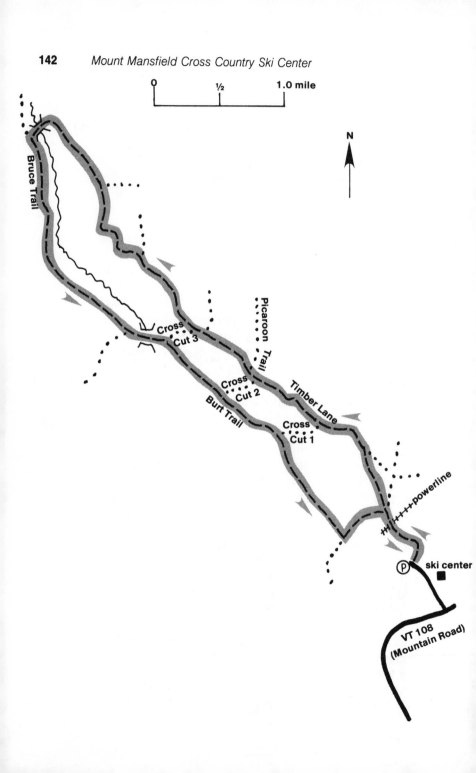

Access

Stowe Village is reached via VT 100. At the four-way stop sign in the village, turn onto VT 108 (known as the Mountain Road) and follow it 7 miles almost to the alpine area. The Cross Country Center is located on the left, just below the Toll House Chairlift, and is well marked.

The Tour

After checking in at the center building, ski down the field, to the left, and up toward the powerline. Where there is a choice of three trails, take the center one. It is labeled Timber Lane and marked as an easy trail. Ski uphill, then along the edge of a hill. At the next intersection, turn left. Continue skiing along the edge of the hill. The next trail to the left is Cross Cut 1; stay on Timber Lane. Above you through the trees is Mt. Mansfield, the "Nose" at 4020 feet, and several ski trails. An open snowfield lies on the opposite side of the ski area. Another Cross Cut trail, numbered 2, leaves left. Stay on Timber Lane and climb to the right more steeply. Picaroon Trail leaves on the right; keep going straight.

There is room to skate on this trail, if that is your technique of choice. Some areas don't allow skating on all their trails because they are too narrow. Continue climbing steeply. The Wedge Trail comes in on the right. In skiing, a "wedge" refers to the snowplow position used in slowing down and turning. Ski back into the woods from a more open area, where there is a mix of hardwoods and softwoods. The brook is now visible on the left below you. The trail sweeps around several corners, not too steeply.

Several woodpecker-ravaged trees stand by the edge of the trail. The chickadees were working the buds on some small bushes along here, apparently finding some nourishment there. The trail bends sharply to the left and over a bridge. On the left you will see a tree with large holes chopped by the pileated woodpecker. These woodpeckers can move an amazing amount of wood in search of bugs under the bark. Ski along the flat to another intersection and turn left on the Bruce Trail, which leads to the Burt Trail. You are about 3 miles from the center. After finishing this tour, another skier in the parking lot mentioned how wonderful the Burt Trail was, and I had to agree with him. The trail is wide, with enough slope to make it fun but not scary.

As you ski along the trail, check the bank along the edge of the brook on your left. Such undercut portions and the caves under the roots of trees are the kinds of places that bears use to hibernate and have their cubs. As the weather warms, they come out in search of food. They sometimes come out even in winter warm spells to check things out.

The brook is good sized and looks like it might hold some fish. Ranch Camp Trail goes off to the right, reaching the Trapp Family Lodge in 2 miles. The Burt Trail continues back to the center. Cross the brook again. Just beyond the bridge on the left is a large boulder with trees growing out of it. Over the years, the roots of trees work down into the rock, allowing water and ice to enter and split it even more. The process may be slow, but eventually big rocks become small ones. At the next intersection, Cross Cut 3 leaves left and climbs steeply. You continue along Burt, passing Cross Cut 2 on the left. In the spring, you can see the Christmas fern, which stays green under the snow, peeking out in sunny spots. Cross Cut 1 goes up to the left, and you continue down very steeply around two corners. Ski with care. There is plenty of room, but the brook lies close to the trail and too much speed could be costly.

The Ranch Valley Trail goes up to the right at the bottom of the hill. Turn left and climb steeply through a sweep-

The Stowe area is blessed with perfect terrain for cross-country skiing

ing turn to the right. At the top, you will see the touring center off to the right across the field.

Other Places to Ski

The Stowe region probably offers a greater variety of outstanding cross-country skiing than any other comparable area in the state. The Trapp Family Lodge on Trapp Hill Road, off the Mountain Road, has nearly forty miles of trails through some of Vermont's most scenic terrain, with memorable views of Mount Mansfield and Smuggler's Notch. The Topnotch Touring Center, also on the Mountain Road, has about twelve miles of novice-to-expert trails. The Catamount Trail crosses the valley, and you can combine the trails of several ski areas in a cross-valley ski experience.

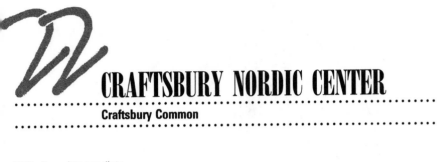

CRAFTSBURY NORDIC CENTER

Craftsbury Common

Difficulty: Intermediate
Distance: 7 miles
Map: Craftsbury Nordic Center Map

Riding up the hill to the village of Craftsbury Common feels like a trip back in time. The town is set around a typical New England green. Trim white houses, a church or two, and a school look no different than they would have one hundred years ago. And the "top of the world" views add to the charm. The particular draw for skiers, of course, is one of the best ski centers in Vermont.

Here you can get an early start to your ski season. Many years the skiing begins during November. Of course, due to its northern location, you can also experience some extreme cold here, but to the skilled Nordic enthusiast, dressing for the occasion is all part of the game.

Craftsbury Nordic Center offers rustic but comfortable lodging and excellent food. It is worth planning your ski day around a luncheon reservation at the touring center.

Access

To get to Craftsbury Common, take VT 15 west from West Danville or east from Morrisville. One mile west of Hardwick or 13 miles east of Morrisville, turn north on VT 14. The signs for Craftsbury Common are at the first paved road to the right, 7 miles up VT 14. After the turn,

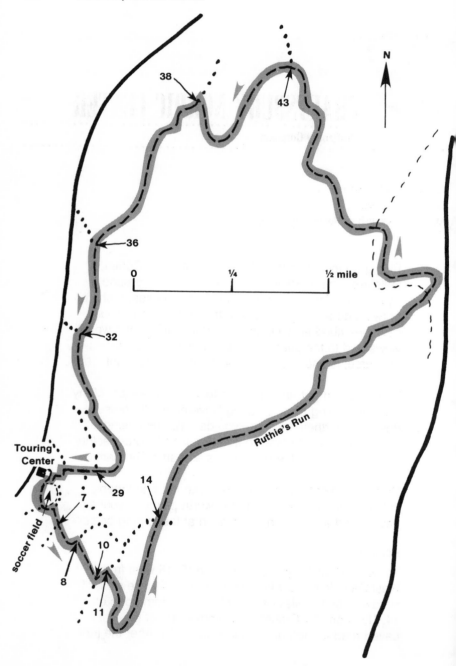

you climb a long hill and pass through the small village of Craftsbury and reach Craftsbury Common three miles after leaving Vt 14. From Craftsbury Common, keep going straight (north) on the main road for .8 mile and take the third right. Follow this road for .5 mile and turn left in the center of Mill Village. Go north for .7 mile, and the turn-off to the Craftsbury Nordic Center will be on your right. From Craftsbury Common, there are signs to the Center at each intersection.

There are several large parking lots. The touring center lodge is located in a small wooden building on your left. Make sure you stop in to get your ticket and to check the wax of the day and current trail conditions.

The Tour

This trail is called Ruthie's Run, about 9 kilometers or 7 miles long. Starting on top of a hill is one of the most attractive things about Craftsbury: Everything starts downhill.

Coming out of the touring center door, note the soccer field on your right. Ski to the field and around the tracks toward a small building opposite the touring center. You will see signs for Ruthie's Run. The intersections are numbered throughout. At number 7, there is a sweeping downhill turn to the left. Go right at number 8. You will notice some markers on the trail that are part of a summer exercise trail. The signs show different exercises to do on each spot.

At intersection 10, go left, and at number 11, go right. The trail goes up and down with easy, swinging corners. At intersection 14, you can return to the center, less than a half mile away, by going left. Since Ruthie's Run goes steeply downhill here, if you are already cold and uncomfortable the trail back might be a good idea. Go straight to continue.

Craftsbury offers touring for all ages

There is a snow depth marker on the right. I was there early in the season on a low snow year, and it already showed two feet of snow. The marker goes to four feet, which is not simply wishful thinking. In an open spot on the left, a dead tree is full of woodpecker holes.

The trail climbs steeply and then gradually. Look under the evergreen trees for animal tracks. You will see squirrel and rabbit tracks here. A sign indicates that it is 5 kilometers (3 miles) back to the center. The trail rolls onto an open field. You can see the old barbed wire fence and a modern electric fence. The long mounds of snow result from the oldest New England fence, the stone wall.

You briefly ski beside a yellow farmhouse and grey barn across a road. Turn back left into the field next to a small pump house. At the edge of the woods, you can see an old metal livestock watering tank.

The trail can be obscured here by blowing snow. Watch for the trail markers: blue diamonds on wooden posts. There are nice views of some rather atypical Vermont mountains from the field. The more usual high peaks have been replaced by soft, rolling mounds tinged in green and grey.

Reenter the woods between a large maple and an old apple tree. A steep downhill ahead is marked with a caution sign. You enter an area of hardwoods after skiing in evergreens. At intersection 43, stay left. You start back into evergreens, in this case, large cedars. This is the edge of a cedar swamp, damp and cool in the summer and protected from the wind in winter. The

Alternating fields and woods are typical of Craftsbury's terrain

trail swings right into an open section of swamp. There are cattails along the edge of a small brook that is bridged by the trail. Leaving the swamp, the trail climbs up and over a glacial esker, a gravel-filled hill left by the last ice age.

At number 38, keep left. It is 1 mile back to the center. Continue along a flat and gradual grade to numer 36, a Y intersection, where you bear left. Bear left again at the next intersection and look for a ski center sign in the trees. At the next intersection, turn left. Very shortly, you come to intersection number 29, where there is a steep downhill with a sharp left turn in an open area, followed by a quick dip. Watch for a large birch tree on your right as you ski up the hill. Climb through a cutover area. Stay left on the main trail. There are scenic views across the valley toward several large and busy looking farms.

The hill you are climbing is the price you must pay for skiing downhill at the beginning of the tour. Keep climbing through large maples. At the top, you will be in the area behind the ski center. Ski up to your left toward the center.

Other Places to Ski

The Craftsbury Nordic Center staff can provide information about backcountry tours on the Catamount Trail, which passes through the Center and just north of the village of Craftsbury Common. Greensboro, 10 miles southeast of Craftsbury Common, offers some 25 miles of trails suitable for all ability levels—about three-quarters of them groomed (see Chapter 23).

HIGHLAND LODGE

Greensboro

Difficulty: Novice
Distance: 3 miles
Map: Highland Lodge Ski Map

Located in northern Vermont, Highland Lodge stands
high above Caspian Lake, an hourglass-shaped lake
that has for many years been a summer mecca for writers and educators. The trail system is extensive, con-
taining some interesting terrain, and the views are great.
The tour I suggest here is an ungroomed loop, which
will give you an opportunity to test your skills without
venturing too far into the wilderness.

The ski center has an interesting note on their map:
"Caution: Trails may have deadfalls, over-hanging
branches, stumps, rocks, streams, sudden dips, turns
and maintenance equipment in your way. Keep a sharp
lookout ahead and always ski so that you can avoid
these and other obstacles!" I couldn't have said it better
myself.

Access

From Hardwick, take VT 15 east 2 miles to VT 16. Turn
left and travel 5 miles to Greensboro Bend, where signs
direct you left to Greensboro—3 miles away. You can
also reach Greensboro from the north by taking VT 16
off I-91 at exit 25 and traveling 15 miles to Greensboro
Bend and the Greensboro access road on the right.
Signs will direct you from Greensboro to Highland

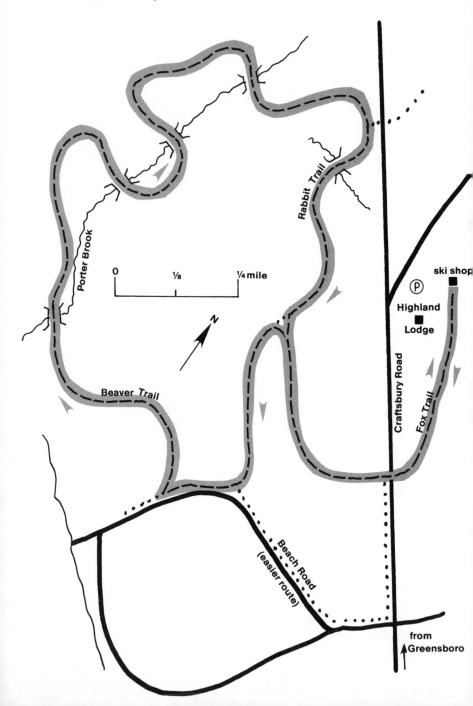

Lodge, which is about 1.5 miles north of the center of town on the paved road to East Craftsbury.

The Tour

All trails start behind the lodge and in front of the ski shop. After paying the trail fee, ski to the left in front of some cabins and above the road. The trail slopes gently to the road. There you have two choices. You can walk down the road to the bottom of the hill, turn right, and ski down Beach Road (the easiest way to start this tour), or, if you appreciate a challenge, you can go directly across the road and angle across the field in front of the tennis court. The trail for the harder route is called Fox Trail. The trail enters evergreens, and there are some nice views across the lake. You swing around the corner to the left at the next intersection. You will see this spot on your return trip.

At the bottom of the hill, you reach Beach Road (if you skied in on the road, here is where the routes converge). Turn right on Beach Road. After a short ski, turn right on Beaver Trail.

Ski to the stream and go across it on a narrow bridge. There are signs on the trees indicating that this stream is a spawning stream and closed to fishing. One of the great northern sports is smelting. In the spring anglers stand on the banks with dip nets and take little fish out by the bucketful. They are so small that they are fried and eaten whole: One of the tastiest of treats.

Continuing, climb slightly out of the swamp and into hardwoods. You are skiing on a small bench above the swamp, next to a ledge on your left—a pretty spot.

Keep skiing until you reach the intersection with Rabbit Trail. Turn right and ski down steeply to a bridge. Swing up and around to the right above the brook. You are

The lodge sits on a ridge above Caspian Lake

now skiing on the other side of the swamp, heading back toward the lodge. The road is visible on the left. I saw some mink sign along one of the brooks here. Keep slabbing along the hill, until you reach the intersection with Fox Trail. Turn left and ski uphill. You will be out of the trees and back at the tennis courts shortly.

Other Places to Ski

The Greensboro area offers some twenty-five miles of ski trails, many marked and maintained, a few unmarked and unmaintained. There are tours suitable for every level of ability and stamina. The best guide to these trails is the map provided by Highland Lodge. Personnel at the lodge can help you select suitable tours. The Craftsbury Nordic Center (see Chapter 22), with over 60 miles of trails and access to the Catamount Trail, is only 12 miles away.

BURKE MOUNTAIN

Burke Mountain Cross

Difficulty: Intermediate
Distance: 8 miles
Location: East Burke

Burke Mountain is located in the "Northeast Kingdom," so named by Vermont governor (and later Senator) George Aiken in a political speech in the 1940s. The "Kingdom" is a high area with several mountains of over three thousand feet, a part of New Hampshire's White Mountain chain. The first ski trails on Burke Mountain were cut by the Civilian Conservation Corp in the 1930s. To give you an idea of how isolated this area has been, the town of Granby did not have electricity until 1963.

Stan Swaim has developed a very nice ski area here. The trails are wide and easy to ski, and you can expect to be treated well. If you get hungry, Vegetarian Chili, usually available on weekends, is the center's specialty. The ski area has snacks and soup available. If you are interested in a special treat, try Bailey's Country Store in East Burke. Their deli is well worth the stop.

Access

From exit 23 on I-91, take VT 5 north through Lyndonville to VT 114 north and east. Follow VT 114 through the village of East Burke. Just past the center of the village, signs for the ski area will tell you to turn right. Follow the signs to the downhill area, and between the two base areas, turn left on a smaller side road, about 1.5 miles from the village. There is a sign for the touring center at the road entrance.

The Tour

After checking in at the lodge, walk to the back of the parking lot. Begin the tour by skiing up on the Candy Bar Hill Trail through evergreens. There are some white cedar trees here, a species not seen in our southern Vermont tours. You may have seen such trees used as foundation plantings around houses. The wood is used in boat building and in covering the ribs in wood and canvas canoes before the canvas goes on. It is very durable and long lasting.

After climbing to a flat section, you will reach intersection 20. Take a right turn onto the New Trail. This route is a flat, beginner's trail through birches. The Burke Mountain Ski Area is visible ahead and above you through the trees. The trail swings easily left and right. At the next trail crossing, numbered 9, ski straight across and slightly downhill on Cutter Trail. You are surrounded by an open area of cut timber. The trail swings around to the left and into small softwoods and moderate-sized hardwoods. On a slight downhill, you will see a troll crossing sign. Perhaps you will even see one skiing ahead of you on the trail. They are very recognizable since they are large and hairy, never ski in skin-tight lycra racing suits, and use old wooden skis. They live under the bridge ahead, which crosses a moderate-sized stream.

Swing hard to the right, then to the left, and climb. At intersection 13, turn left on Parr Meadow. Ski along the edge of an open area. There are some old apple trees here, and if you look left across the valley, you can see some houses.

There is a white house and a brown barn on your right.

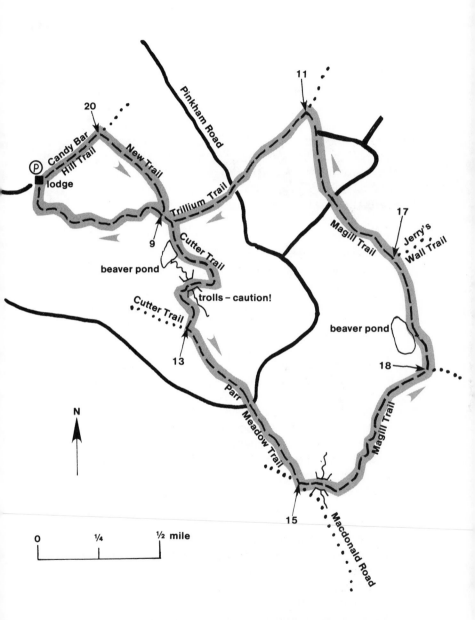

Views from the trails at Burke are generally toward the west

You cross a brook, then travel under a powerline and over a road. After the road, ski up along an open area. There is a brook on the left, and to the right above you, a small bit of the Burke Mountain Ski Area is visible. The trail climbs gradually. You might see a small pump house down the left slope. Climb up steeply to the next intersection, number 15. Turn left onto Magill Trail.

There is a bridge ahead, and the trail slabs along the side of a hill. Nice views of the valley below open up on the left. The trail zigs, zags, and climbs steeply. You pass through small evergreens that darken the area. Even in the winter with all the reflected light off the snow, the evergreens seem to suck up the light and make the area feel colder. They do keep the wild wind from affecting you however. An open, swampy area lies off to the left.

At a Y intersection, numbered 18, stay on Magill. You are about 4 miles from the center. Macdonald goes right. Slab along a hill, then ski to intersection 17. Jerry's Wall goes to the right, but our tour stays on Magill. There are some beautiful views of the valley along here. Look for slippery elm trees; small trees with very striped bark. Ahead is a twisty, difficult downhill with great views if you can slow down long enough to look.

A small camping trailer is visible beyond the road ahead. Cross the road, and at intersection 11, swing sharply left onto the Trillium Trail. The next section is great for double-poling. It rolls just slightly downhill.

Cross another road, and at intersection 9, ski straight onto Cutter Trail on a flat section. There are several sweeping downhill corners ahead. You are now close to the lodge.

A large, broken maple tree is visible in an open area, and around the next corner are several large trailers on the edge of the trail. Ski down to the road and to the lodge, or take your skis off and climb the road to the parking lot.

Other Places to Ski
Your best bet is to combine your tour here with skiing at the Craftsbury Nordic Center or Highland Lodge (see Chapters 22 and 23). Both are an easy drive on good roads. The Burke Mountain staff might know of good local skiing in the backcountry.

HAZEN'S NOTCH X-C SKI CENTER

Montgomery Center

Difficulty: Intermediate
Distance: 6.25 miles
Map: Hazen's Notch X-C Ski Center Map

Located in a wild and uncommercialized part of northern Vermont, Hazen's Notch imparts a feeling of openness to the skier. You feel high above the landscape, skiing on mountaintops. As opposed to Stowe or Waitsfield, lodges are not around every corner, so staying overnight will require some planning, especially during the busy holiday seasons. The skiing is worth any extra effort, however.

The center is small and unassuming, but the trail system is as good as any in Vermont. The trails are laid out in large loops and, according to staff member Rolf Anderson, although the longer trails require a fair amount of time and endurance, a great deal of technique is not needed.

Access

To get to Hazen's Notch X-C Ski Center, drive 12 miles north from Morrisville on VT 100 to Eden. From Eden, take VT 118 north 15 miles to Montgomery Center. (Travelers coming from the nearest I-89 or I-91 exits will approach Montgomery Center from the north on VT 118 or VT 242.) In Montgomery Center, turn east on VT 58. The center is on the left 2 miles out of town. VT 58 is closed

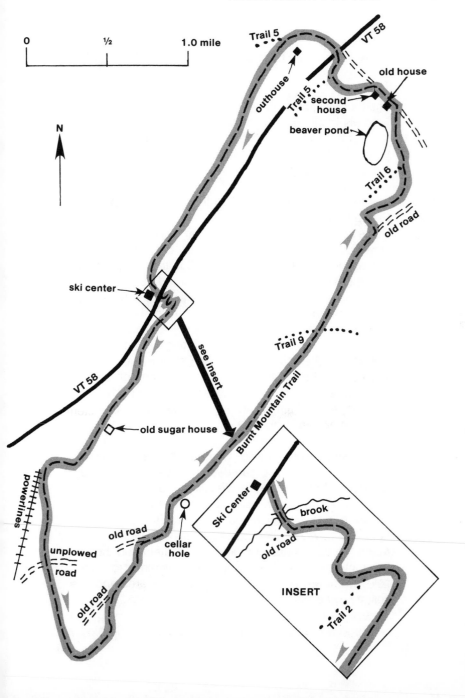

0   ½   1.0 mile

N

Trail 5

VT 58

old house

outhouse

Trail 5

second house

beaver pond

Trail 6

old road

ski center

see insert

Trail 9

VT 58

Burnt Mountain Trail

old sugar house

powerlines

old road

cellar hole

unplowed road

old road

Ski Center

brook

old road

INSERT

Trail 2

to the east of the center in winter, although that fact is
not well indicated by road signs.

The Tour

The tour I describe here is the Burnt Mountain Trail,
which is the longest on the trail map at 6¼ miles (10 kilometers). Skiing time should be several hours or more if
you take time to look at the mountain scenery, a prime
feature of the center.

The trail starts across the road from the center building.
Ski up to and then into a shallow dip over a small brook.
Some of the trees are part of an old apple orchard. The
view across the valley is of Little and Big Jay peaks. You
will be following blue blazes and blue tape strips for the
whole tour. When you reach an old road, turn left onto it
and up the hill. Climb steeply, and swing right and then
back left along the edge of an open field. Trail 2 enters
on the right.

Halfway up the field, turn right and ski into the woods.
The trail climbs steeply, then gradually, through a thicket
of black spruce. Watch and listen for winter birds here—
chickadees and titmice. They seek the protection of
these dense stands of timber.

Ski straight into open woods. There are five massive maples here, and, as you can see, they are all broken and
deformed. You then ski by the ruins of an old sugarhouse. An evaporator, used to boil the sap, is visible on
the left during low snow years. The trail turns sharply
right and downhill, then curves slowly left. When you
reach the powerlines, turn left along a field and then
back into the woods. A red house is visible across the
field. There are some white birches in the area and one
solitary white pine.

Ski uphill and cross an unplowed road. A plastic pipe is

One of the many sugar houses in the Hazen's Notch area

strung through the trees ahead, and several others are visible back in the woods. Ski under the pipe, part of a gravity-fed maple sugar operation. The large maple ahead on the left has taps around the trunk and a thin, plastic tube running down to the larger pipe. A spring weather pattern of freezing nights and warm days starts the maple sap traveling up the tree during the heat of the day and down at night. As it passes the taps, it is forced out and into the tubes. Gravity pulls it downhill to a metal holding tank, where it is collected for boiling.

Continue for some distance, passing an old road that enters from the left, and bear right. There is an old barbed wire fence on your left. Ski gradually downhill. Ruffed grouse tracks are common through this area. The tracks are characterized by a single back toe and three front toes. There were also some deer-rubbed trees along the trail. They rub the fuzz off their antlers in the fall to sharpen them.

Ski through an overgrown field. There are some yellow birches in the area. Swing left and then right past the entrance of another old road on your left and turn sharply left. You are starting to head back toward the center.

An old stone cellar hole lies where another sugarhouse stood. Notice the old apple trees and the grey, wild-looking ledges on the right. The trail swings gradually back to the right and climbs up a slight grade. Watch for a smooth-barked beech tree that has claw marks in it—a series of small holes in the shape of a "C." Bears climb beech trees for their nuts. Ski through an over-grown field and more apple trees. Cross trail number 9; you are now about 3 miles from the lodge. Continue out of the field on an old road; then take a quick uphill out of the road to the left and onto a sloping downhill grade. Soon trail number 6 intersects with yours.

You will soon pass a series of beaver ponds on the left. The second has a new beaver lodge set off from the trail—a smooth, rounded mound of snow. Ski up onto a road which comes in from the right and then bears right past an old house. Down the road is a house trailer and another house. Watch for a trail marker indicating a turn to the left and out of the road. The turn is directly in front of the second house. Ski through a field and swing around to the right. Trail number 5 (the Plateau Track) enters left. There is a sharp left just before the trail crosses a road. Be careful—the road does have traffic.

Across the road, bear left and into a field with a small, outhouse-sized building in the center. Swing left around the building and into the woods. Trail number 5 exits to the right. Part of the trail follows an old power line. The ski center is just ahead.

Other Places to Ski

There is good backcountry skiing not far from the touring center. For an interesting backcountry tour, try Hazen's Notch: Drive to the end of the plowed stretch of VT 58, where you will find limited parking, and ski on a road used by snowmobilers. The Catamount Trail traverses the high terrain just south of Jay Peak; ask the personnel at Hazen's Notch Cross-Country Ski Center for information.

Guidebooks from The Countryman Press and Backcountry Publications

Written for people of all ages and experience, these popular and carefully prepared books feature detailed trail and tour directions, maps and photographs, and notes on points of interest and natural phenomena.

25 Ski Tours in New Hampshire, $8.95

Skating on Skis, $9.95

Runners Guide to Cross-Country Skiing, $10.95

50 Hikes in Vermont, $11.95

25 Bicycle Tours in Vermont, $8.95

25 Mountain Bike Tours in Vermont, $9.95

Vermont: An Explorer's Guide, $16.95

Canoe Camping Vermont and New Hampshire Rivers, $7.95

Backcountry Publications offers many more books on bicycling, hiking, walking, fishing and canoeing in New England, New York state, the Mid-Atlantic states, and the Midwest. These titles are available at bookstores and at certain sporting goods stores or may be ordered directly from the publisher. To order or obtain a complete catalog, write or phone:

The Countryman Press
P.O. Box 175
Woodstock, VT 05091

(802)457-1049.